JENKINS · AMANITA

THE
HOWARD
TILTON
MEMORIAL
LIBRARY

**THE TULANE UNIVERSITY
OF LOUISIANA**

BIBLIOTHECA MYCOLOGICA

Herausgegeben von
J. CRAMER

BAND 57

A Taxonomic and Nomenclatural Study of the Genus *Amanita* Section *Amanita* for North America

by

DAVID T. JENKINS

with 35 plates

1977 · J. CRAMER
In der A.R. Gantner Verlag Kommanditgesellschaft
FL-9490 VADUZ

Author's Address:

Department of Biology
University of Alabama in Birmingham
Birmingham, Alabama 35294

QK
629
.A53J46

© 1977 A.R. Gantner Verlag KG., FL-9490 Vaduz
Printed in Germany
by Strauss & Cramer GmbH, 6945 Hirschberg II
ISBN 3-7682-1132-0

CONTENTS

Introduction 5

Materials, Methods, and Acknowledgements 7

Taxonomic Characters 9
    Fruit body development 9
    Pileipellis 10
    Pileus margin 10
    Pileus trama 11
    Volva 11
    Microscopic characters of the gills 14
    Spores 14
    Stipe 15
    Partial veil 16
    Clamps 17
    Smell and taste 17
    Habitat and distribution 17
    Poisonous taxa 18

The Taxa 20
    Genus *Amanita* 20
    Subgenus *Amanita* 21
    Section *Amanita* 22
    Key to North American Taxa 24
        Amanita agglutinata 27
        Amanita albocreata 29
        Amanita crenulata 31
        Amanita farinosa 33
        Amanita frostiana 35
        Amanita gemmata 38
        Amanita monticulosa 44
        Amanita muscaria 46
        Amanita muscaria var. *muscaria* 46
        Amanita muscaria var. *alba* 50
        Amanita muscaria var. *formosa* 53
        Amanita muscaria var. *flavivolvata* 56
        Amanita muscaria var. *persicina* 59

Amanita pantherina var. *pantherina*	62
Amanita pantherina var. *multisquamosa*	65
Amanita pantherina var. *pantherinoides*	69
Amanita pantherina var. *velatipes*	72
Amanita parcivolvata	75
Amanita wellsii	78
Nomina dubia	79
Type Studies	80
Bibliography	100

In Memory of
My Dad

INTRODUCTION

The name *Amanita* is one of the older mycological names still in use today, reputedly having been derived from the name of Mount Amanon in Cilicia. In the late 1600's and early 1700's the name *Amanita* was applied to the stalked, gill-bearing fungi by Tournefort and Dillenius, while the sessile, dimidiate, gill fungi and woody pore fungi were placed under the name *Agaricus*. Micheli (1729), however, replaced *Amanita* with the name *Fungus* (Donk, 1949). Linnaeus (1737) recognized the importance of gills as a character and chose the name *Agaricus* for this entire group of fungi. The name *Amanita* was infrequently used until 1797 when Persoon reintroduced it for all of the mushrooms that possessed a distinct membranous or friable volva. This grouping, however, included pink as well as white spored specimens. Fries (1815) recognized *Amanita* Pers. in its original sense, but soon reduced it to the rank of "tribus." In doing this he segregated the white and pink spored organisms, with *Amanita* encompassing those with white spores. Credit for publication of *Amanita* as a genus after Jan. 1, 1821 is given to Hooker (Flora Scotica, 1821).

The validity of *Amanita* as a genus has been disputed relatively infrequently since Fries segregated the pink and white spored organisms. Several attempts have been made to segregate *Amanita* into smaller genera, none of which have received continuing support, however (Bas, 1961).

This stability has resulted from an abundance of distinct, diagnostic characters. The prime asset, however, has been the unique combination of these characters, not the individuality of them since several may be found in other genera of agarics. Features such as the volva, annulus, white spores, bilateral gill trama, stipe trama, schizohymenial gill development, and others have in combination delimited a taxon which is quite distinct from other genera of agarics.

Because of this abundance of diagnostic characters, the infrageneric classification of the genus has also undergone numerous changes (Bas, 1969). For the purposes of this study the classification proposed by Corner and Bas (1962) (Fig. 1) is followed. In this classification the amyloidity of the spores (Gilbert and Kuhner, 1928) is used in the separation of two subgenera, subgenus *Lepidella* having amyloid spores and subgenus *Amanita* having inamyloid spores with microscopic features of the volva being a primary subsectional character.

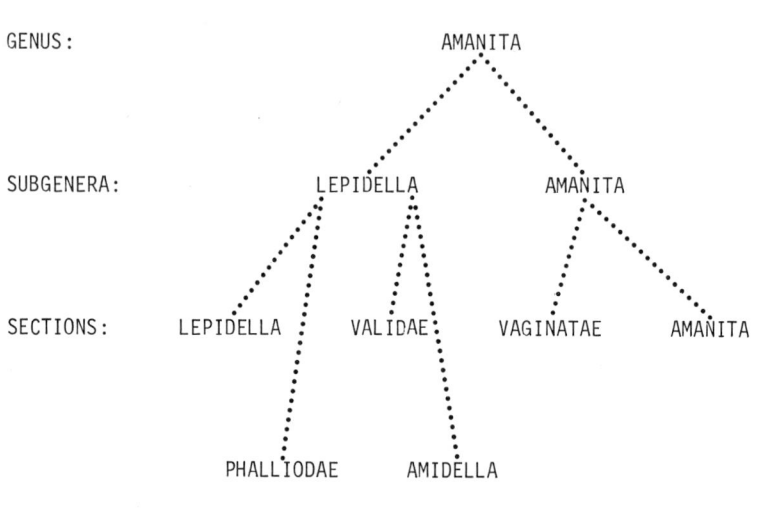

Figure 1. Classification of the genus *Amanita*

In the majority of past taxonomic publications on *Amanita* in North America the diagnostic characters used were usually macroscopic. Rarely were microscopic features used to any extent to define a taxon. More recently, however, microscopic characters have become quite important in the taxonomy of the genus. Dr. Cas Bas (1969), in his monograph of section *Lepidella*, stressed the microscopic features of the volva and defined the potential of other microscopic features in definitive studies.

The use of microscopic characters in the taxonomy of section *Amanita* necessitated a revision of the taxonomic concepts therein. In addition to taxonomic revision, the nomenclature of the taxa was found to be laced with problems. Many of these had their origin in the infrequent typification by past authors such as Peck and Murrill. Occasionally the authors had specified no type specimens, and frequently the citation of specimens was vague. Therefore, several lectotypes and neotypes had to be designated.

It is hoped that the information and adjustments in this study will help stabilize the taxonomy and nomenclature of the section and will facilitate the identification of the taxa therein.

MATERIALS, METHODS, AND ACKNOWLEDGEMENTS

Specimens were examined from the following herbaria and my thanks are extended to the curators: The University of Tennessee (TENN), Dr. L. R. Hesler (emeritus curator); San Francisco State University (abbreviated HDT after the collector) Dr. H. D. Thiers; Plant Pathology Herbarium, Cornell University (CUP and CUP-A), P. M. Fazio; The University of Michigan (MICH), Dr. R. L. Shaffer; The National Fungus Collections (BPI), Dr. P. L. Lentz; The Academy of Natural Sciences of Philadelphia (PH), C. Goulden; The New York Botanical Garden (NY), Dr. C. T. Rogerson; The University of North Carolina (NCU), J. R. Massey; The University of Florida (FLAD), Dr. James W. Kimbrough; Farlow Herbarium, Harvard University (FH), L. I. Nevling, Jr.; The New York State Museum (NYS), Stanley J. Smith; Museum National D'Histoire Naturelle, Laboratoire De Cryptogamie (PC), Dr. Roger Heim; Naturhistoriska Riksmuseet, Stockholm, (S), Carl-Fredrik Lundevall; Rijksherbarium, Leiden (L), Dr. Cas Bas; The University of Copenhagen (CP), Dr. Morten Lange; The University of British Columbia (UBC), Dr. R. J. Bandoni; Plant Research Institute (DAOM), J. A. Parmelee; The University of Alabama in Tuscaloosa (ALU), Elizabeth Sheldon; and the following personal collaborators, Dr. Rolf Singer, Field Museum of Natural History, Dr. A. H. Smith, The University of Michigan, and Dr. Cas Bas, Rijksherbarium, Leiden. A very special note of thanks is extended to Dr. R. H. Petersen and Dr. L. R. Hesler whose advice and guidance were continually available during this study.

I am deeply indebted to several organizations from which funds were received supporting this project: The National Science Foundation, research grant GB-35210, 1972-74; grants from Highlands Biological Station, Highlands, North Carolina, 1971, 1975; Society of Sigma Xi, 1971; and Faculty Research Grants, University of Alabama in Birmingham, 1974-76.

Not all of the taxa discussed herein were observed in the fresh condition, but collections were made from 1970 through 1976. Examinations of all taxa were made on dried, herbarium material. Areas visited for collecting included Alabama, Florida, Georgia, Kentucky, Louisiana, Michigan, Mississippi, North Carolina, South Carolina, Tennessee, Belgium, and Holland.

The characters observed when examining an *Amanita* fruit body, whether fresh or dried, were numerous. These characters were concerned with the size, shape, color, location, texture, disposition, and consistency of various structures of the fruit body. Many features, such as spore print color, macrochemical reactions, colors, and color changes could usually be obtained only from fresh material. For the dried material such data could be obtained only from notes accompanying herbarium specimens. Most herbarium material, however, lacked such data. Most of the dried specimens could be examined, but some of the older or poorly dried collections supplied little information because of the poor reinflation of vital structures. The descriptions below were compiled from: a) fresh and dried specimens personally examined, b) notes and labels accompanying herbarium specimens, and c) published desscriptions and illustrations of taxa included in this study.

All microscopic examinations were made with a Wild Heerbrug M20 research microscope, utilizing both bright field and phase optics, magnifying up to 3125x, and a Treffenberg-type drawing tube. In addition Wild Heerbrug M3, M5, and AO Spencer stereoscopes were used for more exacting macroscopic examinations. Photographs were made with a Nikon FFM-B and M35S camera back and a Nikon FTN with a macro lens.

Reagents used were formulated generally using recipes by Singer (1962) and Bas (1969). These include: 10% NH_4OH in H_2O; 2% KOH (anhydrous) in H_2O; 10% KOH (anhydrous) in H_2O; Melzer's reagent (=KI + I + chloral hydrate + H_2O); 95% ethyl alcohol; ammoniac 1% congo red solution; cotton blue (Kotlaba and Pouzar, 1964). Tissues were examined by free-hand sections using Elderberry pith, the tissue having been soaked for a short period of time in H_2O or in 10% NH_4OH solution, then 95% ethyl alcohol, and finally H_2O. When necessary, fragments were soaked in 10% NH_4OH or H_2O and examined as squashes. For older, poorly dried specimens the soaking time was extended in an attempt to better reinflate the tissues. After examinations were completed in the above processes, the alkaline solution was replaced by ammoniac 1% congo red, heated to evaporation, and replaced by 10% NH_4OH. This process resulted in the cell walls being stained a distinct pinkish-red. All spores were examined in mounts of H_2O, 10% NH_4OH, Melzer's reagent, and cotton blue. All tissues were first examined as thick fragments in order to establish the layering and orientation of elements, after which the tissues were crushed for more qualitative observations.

Colors cited are from Methuen (M), Ridgeway (R), and personal designation. All herbarium abbreviations are from Lanjouw and Stafleu (1964). The following additional abbreviations should be noted: GSMNP = Great Smoky Mountains National Park, spanning North Carolina and Tennessee; HDT = Harry D. Thiers (herbarium housed at San Francisco State University); DTJ = David T. Jenkins (personal herbarium).

TAXONOMIC CHARACTERS

Fruit body development (Illust. plates 13, 14): Included within the development of the *Amanita* fruit body are some very characteristic and/or unique processes (Atkinson, 1909; de Bary, 1866; Reijnders, 1963; Bas, 1969). The formation of the fruit body is hemiangiocarpous, with the lamellae being endogenous until just before sporulation. The lamellar formation is unique to the genus in that these structures do not develop as projections into a preformed cavity, but from primordial tissue between the stipe and pileus as plates of parallel hyphae separated by hymenial palisades. Thus, the gills are bracketed by the pileus trama and the partial veil. This process has been termed "schizohymenial", and, in conjunction with the hemiangiocarpy, the fruit body development is further described as bivelangiocarpic (Reijnders, 1963).

The first structure to differentiate from the primordial tissue is the universal veil or volva. This is followed by the pileus, which in section *Amanita*, is delimited from the volva by a distinct, gelatinous layer (see below). Subsequently, the lamellae are laid down as described above.

In section *Amanita* the fruit body develops nearer the upper surface of the primordial bulb. The tissue nearer the lower surface remains undifferentiated resulting in a distinct basal bulb which is characteristic of this section, separating it from section *Vaginatae* which usually has no distinct bulb.

Initiation of pileus formation is followed by differentiation of the stipe. Bas (1969) described three primary methods by which the stipe elongates: 1) the "apex elongating stipe", 2) the "base elongating stipe", and 3) the "totally elongating stipe." Fruit bodies in section *Amanita* exhibit the "apex elongating stipe." In this development only that part of the stipe above the margin of the primordial cap elongates. The lower part of the stipe and basal bulb rarely participate in the elongation. Stipe elongation is another character that separates sections *Vaginatae* and *Amanita* within the subgenus *Amanita*, with *Vaginatae* having a "totally elongating stipe."

Pileipellis (Illust. plate 15): The pileipellis (Bas, 1969) in section *Amanita* is an ixocutis, existing as a gelatinous layer between the volva and pileus trama. This layer is the result of the rapid gelatinization of the hyphae, which may or may not become totally deteriorated. These hyphae are usually quite slender and sparsely to moderately branched, and their orientation either radial or interwoven. Occasionally this layer is very thin, or almost nonexistent as in A. *farinosa*. In a majority of taxa, however, this layer is well developed, as evidenced by the conspicuous viscidity of the pilei of specimens collected. Environmental conditions have a great influence on this layer. If the humidity is high this layer may be more conspicuous and become so slippery that the volva remains entirely at the base. Low humidity may cause a drying of this layer resulting in greater adherence of the volval material to the pileus surface. Due to this influence of environmental conditions, the adherence of the volval remnants to the pileus surface should be thoroughly studied before being used as a taxonomic character.

Pileus margin: The pileus margin in section *Amanita* is characteristically radially striate, with the degree of striation varying with the taxon. Some taxa, such as A. *wellsii*, are rarely striate at first, but become strongly so with age, while a few taxa, such as A. *pantherina* var. *pantherinoides*, may only become faintly striate. Most are distinctly striate at a very early stage. Several are distinctly tuberculate-striate, as in A. *parcivolvata* and some specimens of A. *gemmata*, and more rarely sulcate-striate, as in A. *farinosa*. These striae correspond to the attachment of the gills on the underside of the pileus. This character is developmentally significant, primarily in allowing rapid expansion of the cap, and as a taxonomic character is very important, especially in conjunction with the amyloidity of the apores. Most taxa which produce inamyloid spores also have marginal, pileus striations.

The presence of these striations appears to be a function of the thickness of the pileus flesh, which in section *Amanita* diminishes rapidly toward the pileus margin. This thin flesh allows observation of the gill connections on the underside of the pileus and permits the "accordion effect" important to the expansion of the young fruit bodies. Occasionally the striations are less developed than normal, and this results from an abnormally thick, pilear flesh.

An appendiculate margin does not appear to be an important character in section *Amanita*. Rarely are specimens found on which remnants of the volva or partial veil extend from the pileus margin. Infrequently specimens of A. *muscaria*, A. *wellsii*, and a few others exhibit this character to a minimum degree. This has no taxonomic value, however.

Pileus trama (Illust. plate 16): The trama of the pileus is composed of irregularly disposed, moderately branched, filamentous hyphae (=feeding hyphae, Bas, 1969) and short, terminal chains of inflated cells (=acrophysalides, Bas, 1975). The filamentous hyphae are usually quite slender, but occasionally slightly inflated. Occasionally small, insignificant numbers of gloeoplerous hyphae may be observed. The inflated cells are usually variable in shape, but a majority appear to be broadly elongate, usually elliptic, oblong-elliptic, fusiform, clavate, or some variation thereof. Rarely can these elements be found as intercalary. Toward the outer surface of the pileus these components usually become much more densely packed, sometimes becoming quite difficult to dissociate. Clamp connections may or may not be found on the filamentous hyphae. These characters seem consistent for all taxa in section *Amanita* with no significant variation.

Volva (Illust. plates 23-35): The volva has long been recognized as one of the major structures distinguishing the genus *Amanita* from most other agarics. In many past taxonomic studies the macroscopic features of this structure have been of primary importance with the microscopic features largely overlooked. Bas (1969) undertook an extensive investigation of section *Lepidella* in which the microscopic structure of the volva was of major taxonomic value. These features are also of importance in the taxonomy in section *Amanita*.

As with many structures of an *Amanita* fruit body, the volva in specimens of this section is composed of branching, filamentous, generative hyphae subtending single or terminal chains of variously shaped, inflated cells. Occasionally gloeoplerous hyphae may also be present, but these have relatively little taxonomic value except in A. *agglutinata* and A. *monticulosa* where they are quite abundant. Hyphal construction in *Amanita* is characteristically monomitic, although I have found skeletal hyphae, or at least skeletalized generatives, in an unidentified specimen of section *Lepidella*.

The types of filamentous hyphae in the volva are of little taxonomic importance, but the relative ratios of filamentous to inflated hyphae is of considerable value. In most cases a decrease in numbers of filamentous hyphae and an increase in numbers of inflated cells results in a more friable volva, as found in section *Amanita*, while the reverse trend produces a more membranous volva, as found in most taxa of section *Vaginatae*. A predominance of chains of inflated cells instead of single, terminal inflated cells also produces a more friable condition. Although most taxa within section *Amanita* have a significant number of filamentous hyphae in the volva, a floccose consistency predominates due to the abundance, size, and disposition of inflated cells.

In addition to numbers, the shape of the inflated cells has taxonomic importance. Thus far in section *Amanita* the shapes have not differed enough among the taxa to warrant division into supraspecific groups, but there are some differences among the individual taxa. The shape of the cells is usually variform, ranging from globose to cylindric with numerous intermediate forms. The majority of inflated cells are usually broadly elliptic, oblong-elliptic, or elliptic, with lesser numbers of globose to subglobose and clavate to cylindric. Usually these cells are found as terminal chains, or rarely intercalary, the chains frequently exhibiting a broadly shaped terminal cell with more elongate subtending cells. Occasionally an inflated cell may be terminal on a filamentous hypha, the shape of the cell varying.

The disposition of these assorted hyphae varies from apicobasal to irregularly interwoven. The volval material on the pileus of A. *farinosa* rarely occurs as distinct warts, but usually as a mealy-pulverulent layer. Here the volva is composed of irregularly interwoven elements. In *A. monticulosa* there are distinct warts on the surface which are composed of apico-basal elements. In taxa where the volva is found as warts near the center and floccose patches on the margin of the cap both orientations can be found.

The layering in the volva of specimens in this section is not very distinct. In none of the specimens examined was the layering distinct, although occasionally the types of cells or number of hyphae in the inner surface appeared slightly different from those of the outer surface. Specimens of *A. pantherina*, *A. agglutinata*, *A. gemmata*, and several others, where a definite, basal, free limb and floccose patches on the pileus are found, show some layering with the volval limb on the base exhibiting a greater number of filamentous hyphae than on the pileus, creating the more coherent structure. In addition the gelatinization of the pileipellis occasionally involves the inner portion of the volva.

The inner limb of the volva, an extension of volval material between the partial veil and stipe, can be demonstrated in most taxa of section *Amanita*. Frequently, as in *A. muscaria* and *A. pantherina* var. *multisquamosa*, the inner limb remains as chunks on the lower, outer edge of the annulus. In most of the other annulate specimens some evidence of the inner limb, usually various inflated cells, can be found on the lower surface of the annulus. In *A. parcivolvata* the abortive annulus material, along with inner limb material, is dispersed over the surface of the stipe.

Not infrequently volval material is located on the stipe, especially on the lower portion. The disposition of volval remnants as ringlets on the lower stipe is characteristic of the members of the *A. muscaria* complex, and is occasionally found in other taxa. This material is very similar to that on the basal bulb, although it may tend to have a smaller proportion of filamentous hyphae. As described by Bas (1969) these ringlets are created by a continued elongation of the stipe after the volva stops growing. A continued thickening of the stipe may cause a longitudinal disruption of these rings. One must not be fooled, however, by the occasional splitting of the stipe tissue to form similar recurved, ascending rings.

Microscopic characters of the gills (Illust.plates 17-19): Microscopic examination of the gills reveals several obvious features, only a few of which, however, seem of significant taxonomic value. At the generic level the bilateral gill trama is of utmost importance. This character links *Amanita* with the genus *Limacella* in the *Amanitaceae*, at least during the earlier stages of development, after which the latter develops a trama which is more interwoven. Thus far no specimens of *Amanita* have been found to vary from the bilateral orientation.

In section *Amanita* the trama is composed of diverging hyphae, usually slender and moderately branched, and producing the cells of the subhymenium. Some of the tramal hyphae, however, terminate in single or terminal rows of inflated, elongate cells which do not connect with the hymenium. These cells usually dominate the appearance of the tissue, as is often the case in other structures in *Amanita* fruit bodies, and may be oblong-elliptic to cylindric in shape. The trama tissues diverge from a mediostratum, curving downward and out toward the subhymenium. Occasionally gloeoplerous hyphae may also be found.

The subhymenium invariably appears as ramose to inflated ramose (Bas, 1969), the cells of the subhymenium being rather slender and branched. More frequently than not the dried specimens studied were either very old or poorly dried, preventing sufficient reinflation for accurate study. Little taxonomic importance was placed on this character.

The basidia have very little or no taxonomic value in this section. Size and shape vary with a taxon, although the general shape is usually long and slender, perhaps correlated to the ramose subhymenium (Bas, 1969). Basidia are usually 4-sterigmate, although occasionally two- and rarely one-sterigmate basidia are observed.

Spores (Illust. plate 20): One of the most important features resulting from microscopic analysis of the lamellae concerns the spores. The reaction of the spore wall to Melzer's reagent is negative, a character which partially defines the subgenus *Amanita*.

For the separation of individual taxa importance was placed on the shape and size of the spores. For this analysis the standards of l/b ratio established by Bas were employed, with E substituted for the l/b ratio and $\underline{E^m}$ for the average l/b ratio, following Corner (1947).

The shape of the spores in this section ranged from globose to elongate, with an $\underline{E}$ value from 1.0 to 2.0. Several taxa had very characteristic $\underline{E^m}$ values, A. *albocreata*, A. *crenulata*, and A. *frostiana* having values within the globose to subglobose range and A. *agglutinata*, A. *parcivolvata*, and A. *wellsii* having values near 2.0, or elongate to cylindric. Most of the other taxa fell within a range of approximately 1.2-1.7.

Spore prints of all taxa in this section are white, with only an occasional cream tint.

Spore contents are subgranular to guttulate-refractive. Quite frequently the spores were more often subgranular in the fresh condition, but seemed to undergo a coalescence when heated during one of the staining procedures. This particular trait was consistent throughout the section and could not be used as a delimiting character.

Spore walls are thin and always appear to be smooth. Never was there any ornamentation observed of the type mentioned by Bas (1969).

Within this section the apiculus was of two shapes, cylindric or truncate-conic (conical with a blunt tip). Unfortunately, these shapes were not always consistent within a taxon. Frequently, however, there were trends toward one or the other of these shapes, but never to the degree allowing for its use as a delimiting character.

Stipe (Illust. plate 21): The characters of the stipe in section *Amanita* are relatively constant, with the stipe usually long and slender, almost always as long or longer than the width of the pileus, tapering toward the apex, but with the apex usually slightly expanded. The stipe tissues are always easily separable from the pileus trama at the stipe apex. The surface texture may vary from almost glabrous to lacerate-scaly, but is fairly consistent within the same taxon. The stipe is either hollow or stuffed with moderately branched, filamentous hyphae. The color is usually white to creamy-white, infrequently having a darker color.

Microscopically, specimens of the entire genus exhibit a type of tissue which, in agarics, has been found elsewhere only in the genus *Limacella*, a close relative of *Amanita* (Hoffman, 1861; Boudier, 1886), and in the gasteromycete *Torrendia* (Bas, 1975). This tissue is composed of longitudinally oriented, slender, sparsely to moderately branched, inconspicuous, filamentous hyphae with large, terminal, inflated cells. The inflated cells, frequently clavate to elliptic, usually dominate the appearance of the tissue, although there is usually a considerable number of filamentous hyphae present. In no instance were the cells poorly differentiated as found in some taxa of section *Lepidella* (Bas, 1969). The number of inflated cells often varies with each specimen and in this study was found to have only minor taxonomic value. Rarely do these inflated cells appear as terminal chains, usually being single. Size is also quite variable, some being short and broad and others long and slender, the length ranging from approximately 150-600 μ.

Partial veil (Illust. plate 22): The partial veil or annulus has always been recognized as an important taxonomic character in the genus *Amanita*. The characters employed were almost always macroscopic, i.e., size, shape, color, texture, location, and, more importantly, the presence or absence (Bas, 1969).

In section *Amanita* features of the annulus are not used to delimit groups of taxa, but they do have taxonomic significance for certain individual taxa. In some species, such as *A. parcivolvata* and *A. farinosa*, the annulus is fugacious, and its absence if recognized as a diagnostic character. In *A. wellsii* and *A. crenulata* the partial veil is evanescent, rarely present in mature specimens, occasionally adhering to the pileus margin. Finally, in some taxa, such as *A. gemmata*, an annulus is usually present, but occasionally may be lacking. The location on the stipe has only minor taxonomic significance .g., the median to inferior position in *A. pantherina* var. *velatipes*. In several taxa, such as *A. pantherina* var. *multisquamosa* and *A. muscaria*, the annuli are characteristically thickened on the margin due to the adherence of the inner limb material to the underside. Atkinson (1900) described *A. velatipes* (=*A. pantherina* var. *velatipes*) as having an unique annulus formation in which the veil was formed by the tearing up of the outer layer of the stipe as it elongated. My microscopic examination did not confirm this, however.

In section *Amanita* the microscopic structure of the annulus was fairly consistent and, therefore, had little taxonomic importance. The upper surface was usually composed of narrow, moderately branched, filamentous hyphae frequently with single, terminal, usually elongate, inflated cells. The numbers of cells present varied, and I have not as yet found any consistency within each taxon. The lower surface may resemble very much the upper surface, or there may be an abundance of inflated cells resembling those of the volva.

Clamp connections: The presence or absence of clamps has only minor taxonomic significance in this section. In many of the taxa clamps could be observed in several tissues, but not with any consistency. Clamps were occasionally found at the base of the basidia in a number of taxa, but rarely in abundance. It must be noted, however, that most observations were made on dried herbarium material making reinflation of the tissues frequently difficult.

Smell and taste: Thus far smell and taste have had absolutely no taxonomic importance in this section. The taste and smell are mild in all specimens and can probably best be desscibed as being fungoid. Possible exceptions may be cited from Murrill (1920), who described A. *wellsii* as "tasting mild but with a lingering unpleasantness." Peck (1900) said of A. *crenulata*, "it has reportedly been eaten without harm and to be of an excellent flavor." None of the specimens which I personally collected had any distinctive taste or smell.

Habitat and distribution: Specimens in section *Amanita* are terrestrial and occur primarily in forested areas, more frequently where there is sparse ground cover. A much smaller number can be found growing in open meadows and fields, lawns, and grasslands, e.g., A. *parcivolvata* and A. *farinosa*. The fruit bodies are usually solitary or subgregarious. It is generally recognized that those growing in the woodlands are obligately mycorrhizal (Hatch and Hatch, 1933; Hacskaylo, 1971). Smith (1971) recognizes approximately 75 taxa as ectomycorrhizal. Some taxa are quite exacting in their mycorrhizal relationships, whereas others appear capable of establishing affinities with several types of trees. The mycorrhizal specificity of *Amanita* may not, however, be as great as many have indicated. Many taxa can be found in coniferous and deciduous forests (Hacskaylo, 1971). In the higher mountain ranges there are a few species which may venture above the timber line or exist in other treeless areas, such as grass or heath balds. These, however, are possibly mycorrhizal with some of the other vegetation.

Due to this preference for a mycorrhizal relationship, many taxa in North America are more frequently found in the damp, forested areas, such as the northeastern and southeastern mountainous regions, parts of the gulf coastal area, and the northwestern and southwestern mountainous locales. There are, of course, other areas which possess an obvious *Amanita* flora.

Poisonous taxa: Within the section *Amanita* are several taxa which have been reported to induce intoxication. Included among these are *A. muscaria, A. pantherina, A. pantherina* var. *multisquamosa,* (=*A. cothurnata*), *A. crenulata, A. gemmata,* and *A. frostiana*. Of these only a few have been intensively studied in an attempt to isolate and identify the causative agents.

A large protion of *Amanita* toxicology studies have been directed at *A. muscaria* and *A. pantherina*. Both of these taxa, especially *A. muscaria,* have long histories concerning their intoxicating properties (Tyler, 1958; Benedict, Tyler, Brady, 1966; Tyler, 1962; Wasson, 1968). Much effort has been directed toward isolating and identifying the compounds causing the typical responses. Onda (1964) isolated a substance which produced death in flies after consumption of the mushroom. Takemoto et al. (1964) identified this substance as ibotenic acid, an isoxazole derivative. Another active substance, later named muscimol (Muller et al., 1965; Good et al., 1965), was shown to be a decarboxylated derivative of ibotenic acid. These compounds were related to the typical intoxicating responses of *A. muscaria* by Eugster et al., (1965).

A number of deaths by mushroom poisoning in the past have been attributed to the consumption of *A. muscaria* fruit bodies. *Amanita pantherina* was infrequently thought to be responsible (Krieger, 1921). A study by Benedict, Tyler, and Brady (1966) showed that fruit bodies of *A. pantherina* possessed nearly three times as much of the same toxins as did three varieties of *A. muscaria* individually compared, thus indicating a greater toxic potential in *A. pantherina* (Gilbertson, 1966). Through personal communication, however, I have learned that in the western states specimens of both of these taxa are frequently consumed purposely for their toxic stimulation, no one apparently being concerned with the possibility of death.

Additional taxa within section *Amanita* have been investigated for their possession of ibotenic acid and muscimol. *Amanita pantherina* var. *multisquamosa* has been considered poisonous by several authors (Murrill, 1916; Heim, 1963; Dearness, 1935). Analysis of members of this taxon by Benedict et al. (1966) produced negative results concerning the presence of ibotenic acid or muscimol. More recently, however, investigations by Chilton & Ott (1976) and Pollock, Jenkins, & Chilton (manuscript in preparation) have discovered both ibotenic acid and muscimol in specimens of this taxon. The specimens examined had been collected within the last year, whereas those used by Benedict et al. were over two years old.

A similar situation exists for specimens of A. *gemmata* examined. Benedict et al. found no toxins in specimens identified as A. *gemmata*. There were, however, a number of unidentified specimens, thought to be hybridized color forms of A. *pantherina* and A. *gemmata*, that did possess quantities of toxins intermediated to the amounts found in A. *pantherina* and A. *gemmata*. The studies of Chilton & Ott, and Pollock, Jenkins, & Chilton have revealed positive results on a west coast specimen and negative results on an eastern specimen. These varying results certainly indicate the necessity for continued investigations.

Members of A. *frostiana* have also been considered as being poisonous (Atkinson, 1900; Coker, 1917). This could be due, however, to the superficial resemblance to A. *muscaria*, and, therefore, misidentification of specimens examined. Chilton and Ott have examined a six-year old specimen of A. *frostiana* and found no traces of toxins. The age of this specimen, however, allows for some doubt of its toxicity.

A specimen of A. *pantherina* var. *velatipes* from North Carolina has been found to possess muscimol, indicating the presence of ibotenic acid in fresh specimens (Pollock, Jenkins, & Chilton, manuscript in preparation).

Finally, there are a few reports that describe cases of poisoning by mushrooms tentatively identified as A. *crenulata* (Buck, 1965, 1969).

Macroscopically and microscopically the taxa within section *Amanita* are quite similar. Several taxa have been definitely shown to possess intoxicating substances. With the possibility of hybridization within this group, as mentioned above, it might be advisable not to eat any specimens that can be identified as belonging to this section.

THE TAXA

Amanita Pers. per Hook. 1821. Fl. Scot. 2: 19, May.
    ≡ [*Amanita* Pers. 1797. Tent. Disp. Meth. Fung.: 65, deval. name].
    ≡ *Agaricus* trib. *Amanita* (Pers.) per Fr. 1821. Syst. Mycol. 1: 12.
    (non [*Amanita* Dill. 1719. Cat. Pl. Giessa.: 177, deval. name]; non *Amanita* (Dill.) Rafin. 1830. Medic. Fl. N. Amer.: 189).
= *Pseudofarinaceus* O. Kuntze. 1891. Rev. Gen. Plant. 2: 867.

    Lectotype (Clements & Shear, 1931): *Amanita muscaria* (L. per Fr.) Hook.

    Fruit body agaricoid, fleshy, stipe central, small to large, solitary to subgregarious, primordium enveloped by a membranous or friable volva which, upon expansion of fruit body, ruptures, leaving a membranous sac at base of stem or breaking up into warts, patches, rings, scales, or powder on pileus and/or stipe. Pileus with margin smooth, then spores usually amyloid, or radially striate/sulcate, then spores usually nonamyloid, pileipellis weakly to strongly differentiated, dry to viscid, volva remnants more or less adnate when dry, detersile when viscid. Lamellae usually free, more rarely adnate or narrowly adnexed, edges granular to floccose; lamellulae scarce to very abundant, truncate to attenuate, varying in length, not branched, rarely anastomosing. Stipe cylindrical or attenuate upward, solid, stuffed or hollow, with or without a small to very large, basal bulb. Partial veil present, occasionally fugacious or evanescent, usually forming submembranous to membranous ring or fibrillose, floccose, or pulverulent remnants on stipe, edge of pileus and edges of lamellae. Flesh firm to soft, usually white or whitish, sometimes changing to pinkish, reddish, purplish, brownish, grayish, yellowish, or greenish when exposed, very rarely lactescent.

    Spores small to very large, globose to bacilliform, frequently adaxially flattened, thin walled to slightly thick walled, usually smooth, very rarely minutely verrucose or striolate, without germ pores, mostly white, sometimes cream, buff, olive-buff, yellowish-green in spore prints, with amyloid or nonamyloid walls, rarely with more or less dextrinoid contents, very rarely with small, amyloid warts. Basidia clavate, mostly 4-spored, sometimes 1-, 2-, or 3-spored, clamps present or absent at basal septum. No true cystidia, rarely laticiferous pseudocystidia present. Edges of lamellae sterile, frequently covered with inflated cells or hyphae being remnants of tissue between gills and partial veil. Lamellar trama bilateral, with or without divergent, large, terminal, inflated cells; subhymenium well developed, ramose to cellular. Pileipellis consisting of interwoven to radial, repent, filamentous hyphae frequently gelatinizing; pigment, if present, usually intracellular. Volva composed of irregularly disposed, periclinal, or anticlinal, filamentous hyphae and/or variously shaped, inflated, terminal or catenulate cells. Trama of stem consisting of longitudinal, branching, filamentous hyphae and sparse to very sparse to very abundant, medium to large, slenderly clavate, longitudinal, terminal cells or short, terminal rows of such cells. Clamps in fruit body abundant, scarce or absent.

Habitat: Terrestrial, mostly in forests, frequently forming ectomycorrhiza with trees or shrubs, or rarely in open fields.

Subgenus Amanita:
= Amanita subgen. Vaginaria Forq. 1888. Champ. Sup.: 45, (not val. publ.); ex Quel. 1888. Fl. Mycol. France: 302.
= Amanita subgen. Amanitopsis (Roze) Lange. 1915. Dansk. Bot. Ark. 3(3): 6.
= Amanita subgen. Euamanita Vesely. 1933. Ann. Mycol. 31(4): 212.
= Amanita subgen. Amanitaria (Gilb.) Gilbert. 1941. Not. Amanites 30(2).
= Amanita subgen. Amanitella (Earle) Gilbert. 1918. Genera Amanita: 156.
= Amanita subgen. Peplophora Quelet. 1888. Fl. Mycol. France: 313.

Pileipellis lightly to strongly gelatinized and whitish to brightly colored. Margin of pileus radially striate to sulcate. Lamellae usually white, occasionally cream to yellowish, pinkish, tannish, or grayish. Lamellulae usually truncate. Partial veil membranous, evanescent, or fugacious. Stem stuffed or hollow; flesh rarely changing color upon exposure. Spores globose to cylindrical, nonamyloid.

Observations: The epithet Amanita must be used for this subgenus because the type species of the genus Amanita is found in this group (Lanjouw, 1966; Art. 22).

The infrageneric classification by Corner and Bas accommodates very well the related specimens within the subgenus Amanita. The three primary characters delimiting this group are very consistent among the taxa. The spores are always nonamyloid, the lamellulae truncate to a large degree, and the margin of the pileus is usually striate to striate/sulcate at some period of its development. Similarities can be seen between the taxa of the two subgenera, but the constancy of the above mentioned characters appears to delimit two, natural groups.

Section Amanita:
= Amanita sect. Leucospori Mlady. 1838. Synop. Amanit.: 15.
= Amanita sect. Muscariae (Fr.) Quelet. 1872. Mem. Soc. Emul. Montbeliard, ser. II. 5: 67.
= Amanita sect. Pulveratae Imai. 1933. Bot. Mag., Tokyo 47: 430.
= Amanita sect. Amanitaria (Gilb.) Konr. and Maubl. 1948. Agaricales: 59.
= Amanita sect. Muscariae Fr. 1854. Monogr. Amanitarum Sueciae: 6.
= Amanita sect. Annulati Morgan. 1887. Jour. Mycol. 3(3): 25.
= Amanita sect. Circumscissae Quelet. 1888. Fl, Mycol France: 304.
= Amanita sect. Marginatae Schroet. 1889. Kryptog. Fl. Schlesein. 3(1): 679.
= Amanita sect. Ovisporae Lange. 1915. Dansk. Bot. Ark. 2(3): 5, 8.
= Amanita sect. Floccosae Gilbert. 1918. Genre Amanita: 81, 172.

= *Amanita* sect. *Amanitellae* (Earle) Gilbert. 1918. Genre *Amanita*: 156, 173.

Margin of the pileus striate to striate/sulcate, rarely appendiculate. Pileipellis differentiated as an ixocutis, whitish, pale to darker browns and yellows, to brighter oranges and reds, rarely grayish. Volva usually white or cream, occasionally pale yellow or tan, rarely gray or gray-brown, pulverulent or disposed as floccose warts, scales, patches, ringlets, or crusts on pileus, stipe or basal bulb, occasionally completely disappearing from stipe or bulb, occasionally circumscissle, leaving a slight, floccose-membranous limb on basal bulb. Lamellae usually white, occasionally cream to pale yellow or pinkish. Lamellulae concavely to convexly truncate. Partial veil membranous to evanescent to fugacious, in the latter case frequently leaving pulverulent material on stipe. Stipe usually attenuate upward, occasionally cylindrical, rarely attenuate downward, basal bulb small to large, occasionally marginate, rarely subradicate, stuffed to hollow. Flesh rarely coloring yellowish upon exposure. Smell and taste fungoid, rarely distinct.

Basidia with or without clamps. Hyphae of lamellar trama usually with terminal, inflated cells; hyphae of subhymenium ramose to slightly inflated. Pileipellis composed of repent, subradial to interwoven, filamentous hyphae. Volva composed of irregularly disposed to anticlinal, catenulate or terminal, inflated cells, and scarce to abundant, filamentous hyphae. Clamps in tissues of fruit body variable. Spores small to occasionally large, globose to cylindrical, thin walled, white to pale creamy in spore print, nonamyloid, walls smooth.

Habitat and distribution: Terrestrial in forests and, occasionally, open fields, from cold to temperate to tropical climates.

Observations: The name *Amanita* must be used for this group because it includes the type species of the genus *Amanita*.

Section *Amanita* is separated from section *Vaginatae* by having a bulbous base and a volva that is friable or occasionally limbate. The taxa have nonamyloid spores as do the taxa of section *Vaginatae*.

Section *Amanita* appears to be a very homogeneous group of

organisms. The general stature of the fruit bodies is shared by the A. *muscaria*, A. *pantherina*, and A. *gemmata* complexes, as well as several other taxa, and it is often quite difficult to immediately identify a specimen from a black and white photograph due to this similarity. The disposition of the volval elements is variable because the gelatinous pileipellis, which is highly affected by humidity, allows for great differences in the positioning and character of the remnants on the pileus. The disposition of the volva at the base is usually distinct, but due to the usually floccose texture is easily influenced by environmental factors. The presence or absence of the partial veil seems to be variable, with the annuli of most taxa relatively delicate, occasionally being fugacious, evanescent, or persistent within the same taxon.

Key to the Taxa of Section *Amanita* in North America:

1. Universal veil at stipe base usually pulverulent to delicate floccose, rarely forming a free limb, evanescent ---------- 2
1. Universal veil at base usually forming some type of subappressed to adnate free limb or rings of volval material on bulb, often extending up lower part of stipe -------------- 6

    2. Spores globose to elliptic --------------------------- 3
    2. Spores elliptic to elongate -------------------------- 5

3. Universal veil on pileus having large numbers of gloeoplerous hyphae; pileus areolate; annulus thick and persistent - ------------------------------------- 7. *Amanita monticulosa*
3. Universal veil on pileus having few gloeoplerous hyphae; pileus not aroelate; annulus usually wanting -------------- 4

    4. Volva as gray-brown pulverulence, occasionally forming small, delicate warts -------------------- 4. *Amanita farinosa*
    4. Volva as white floccose warts or patches ----------------
                                          3. *Amanita crenulata*

5. Evanescent annulus produced, usually adhering to margin of pileus leaving only delicate ring on stipe; stipe furfurace-

ous above annulus but nearly glabrous below; pileus zinc orange to ochraceous salmon, occasionally fading to antimony yellow on margin ------------------- 11. *Amanita wellsii*
5. No annulus present; stipe usually covered with yellow pulverulence; pileus usually crimson to deep orange on disc, becoming yellow-orange to golden yellow on margin --- 10. *Amanita parcivolvata*

6. Spores globose to subglobose; $\underline{E}^m$ value <1.2 ----------- 7
6. Spores broadly elliptic to elongate; $\underline{E}^m$ value >1.2 --- 8

7. Fruit bodies 6-15 cm high; pileus white with occasional pale yellow tint; exannulate; stipe white; volva white -- 2. *Amanita albocreata*
7. Fruit bodies 2-7 cm high; pileus bright orange to yellow; annulus usually present; stipe white to yellow; volva yellow -- 5. *Amanita frostiana*

8. Universal veil disposed as ringlets on upper part of basal bulb and lower stipe, or if bulb and stipe naked, then pileus yellow-orange to orange-red -------------- 9
8. Universal veil concentrated on the basal bulb as an inrolled collar or other free margin, or if also found on lower stipe, then as irregular patches or rarely as ringlets --- 13

9. Pileus white to silvery-buff -- 8b. *Amanita muscaria* var. *alba*
9. Pileus some shade of yellow-orange to orange-red to crimson --- 10

10. Pileus maize yellow to yellow-orange, pastel-red, or melon on disc and pale yellow on margin; universal veil pale buff to yellowish-tan to tan ------------------- 11
10. Pileus blood red to orange-red, orange, or yellowish-orange; universal veil white to pale cream-yellow to golden-yellow ------------------------------------ 12

11. Pileus maize yellow to yellow-orange; gills white; universal veil pale buff to pale tan - 8d. *Amanita muscaria* var. *formosa*

11. Pileus pastel-red to melon on disc, pale yellow on margin; gills pale creamy-pink; universal veil yellowish-tan to tan ------------------------- 8e. *Amanita muscaria* var. *persicina*

    12. Volval material white; basidia and subhymenium infrequently clamped ------ 8a. *Amanita muscaria* var. *muscaria*
    12. Volval material yellow; basidia and subhymenium abundantly clamped -- 8c. *Amanita muscaria* var. *flavivolvata*

13. Abundant gloeplerous hyphae in pileus volval remnants; pileus areolate -------------------------- 1. *Amanita agglutinata*
13. Gloeoplerous hyphae rare in volva on pileus; pileus not areolate-- 14

    14. Pileus white or whitish with occasional brownish or yellowish tint on disc; $\underline{E}^m$ value <1.25 --------------------- ---------------- 9b. *Amanita pantherina* var. *multisquamosa*
    14. Pileus yellow to yellow-brown to some shade of brown; $\underline{E}^m$ value >1.25 --------------------------------------- 15

15. Pileus creamy-yellow, pale yellow, golden yellow, occasionally champagne; volva at stipe base usually detersile or subappressed, rarely adnate; pileus margin frequently tuberculate-striate ------------------------ 6. *Amanita gemmata*
15. Pileus yellow-brown to some shade of brown; volva at base usually adnate, forming slight free margin or more frequently cothurnate or ocreate; pileus margin faintly to strongly striate, but rarely tuberculate ----------------- 16

    16. Volva not cothurnate or with thick, free margin, but usually peronate with slight, thin free margin; pileus color usually melleous to dark melleous on margin with chestnut to melleous-avellaneous disc; fruit body not over 10 cm high ------------------------------------- ---------------- 9c. *Amanita pantherina* var. *pantherinoides*
    16. Volva cothurnate or with thick, free margin; pileus color either some shade of brown or mostly yellow with a brownish disc; fruit bodies 5-20 cm high ----------- 17

17. Pileus hair brown to umber to champagne or ivory on disc

with rest of pileus being butter yellow to light yellow to cream, mature fruit bodies medium to large rarely under 10 cm high; spores 6.3-7.9 x 8.7-11 ($\underline{E}^m$ = 1.42) -------------- ----------------------- 9d. *Amanita pantherina* var. *velatipes*

17. Pileus blackish-brown, soot-brown, to olivaecous-brown, becoming paler brown toward margin, rarely melleous; fruit bodies small to large, 4-18 cm high; spores (6.3)7-9.4(10.2) x (7.9)9.4-12.5(13.9) ($\underline{E}^m$ = 1.32) ----- 9a. *Amanita pantherina*

1. *Amanita agglutinata* (Berk. & Curt. in Berk.) Lloyd. 1898. Volvae: 9.

≡ *Agaricus agglutinatus* Berk. & Curt. in Berk. 1849. Hook. Jour. Bot. 1: 97-98.

≡ *Amanitopsis agglutinatus* (Berk. & Curt. in Berk.) Sacc. 1887. Syll. Fung. 5: 23.

≡ *Vaginata agglutinata* (Berk. & Curt. in Berk.) Kuntze. 1898. Rev. Gen. Plant. 3: 539.

Holotype: South Carolina, viii. 1847, M. A. Curtis 1322 (K) [!].

Fruit bodies small, slender, solitary. Pileus approximately 2.5-5 cm diam, hemispherical becoming plano-convex to plane, margin striate-sulcate, white, viscid, areolate; volval remnants areolate-squamose. Lamellae white, broad, ventricose, rounded behind, free, crowded; lamellulae truncate. Stipe 1-3.5 x 0.3-0.7 cm, tapering slightly upward, slightly expanded at apex, stuffed, subfibrillose, basal bulb globose to subglobose; volva appressed against base of stipe, irregularly lobed rim at margin of bulb, 2-2.5 mm deep. Annulus wanting. Flesh rather thin, tapering toward but terminating short of pileus margin.

Hyphae of pileipellis 3-8 µ diam, interwoven, slightly gelatinized, with a significant number of gloeoplerous hyphae. Lamellar trama bilateral, consisting of undifferentiated hyphae and inflated, elongate cells. Remnants of volva on pileus a fairly dense tissue of irregularly disposed, terminal, inflated cells and short, terminal chains of inflated cells; cells broadly elliptic to ovoid, up to 45 x 57 µ and oblong-elliptic, elliptic, and irregularly elongate, up to 15 x 95 µ usually with subtending cells being elongate; hyphae abundant, 4-6 µ diam, moderately branched, clamps not observed, gloeoplerous hyphae abundant; volval cells at the stipe base primarily clavate to elliptic, up to 35 x 75 μ with broadly elliptic cells up to 55 x 70 μ, usually in short, randomly oriented chains; hyphae approximately 5 μ diam, moderately branched, clamps not observed, with gloeoplerous hyphae abundant. Stipe trama hyphae 2-6.5 μ diam, abundant, sparsely branched; inflated cells up to 55 x 145 μ with a tendency to be very short and broad, oblong-elliptic to clavate, terminal, longitudinally oriented. Surface of stem with longitudinal to interwoven gloeoplerous hyphae, often densely branched.

Spores 5.5-8 x 9-12.5 μ, (E = 1.40-1.90; E^m = 1.62), elliptic to elongate, adaxially flattened, smooth, thin walled, hyaline, spore print color white, nonamyloid; contents guttulate to subgranular; apiculus sublateral, cylindric to truncate-conic, up to 2.5 μ in length.

Habitat and distribution: Terrestrial, on ground in sandy woods, late summer, South Carolina.

Collections examined:

United States:
South Carolina - viii. 1847, M. A. Curtis 1322 (K).

Observations: The holotype was the only specimen of this taxon which could be located. Although several herbarium specimens were labeled as *Amanita agglutinata*, they represented misapplications.

Specimens from the eastern United States to which the name *A. agglutinata* has been applied are definitely not the same as the taxon described by Berkeley and Curtis (1849). The primary difference is that *A. agglutinata* has nonamyloid spores while these other specimens have amyloid spores. In addition, the original description of *A. agglutinata* depicts the pileus as being white. The type specimen also has a basal volva with a small, free limb. The specimens to which the name has been frequently applied have pilei with a brownish to pinkish-brown disc and volval remnants as brownish to pinkish-brown scales or patches. The volva at the base is usually very large, thick, and membranous.

This misapplication seems to have been strongly influenced by a publication of Murrill (1913) in which he synonymized *Vaginata agglutinata* with Peck's *Agaricus volvatus*. He described the pileus of *A. agglutinata* as dull white or yellowish to reddish-brown. This aberrant concept was perpetuated by Coker (1917) in which he described the pileus as white to reddish-brown with reddish-brown scales. Included in the article was a photograph which distinctly showed the characters described.

The specimens so described by Murrill and Coker are probably *Agaricus volvatus* Pk. This conclusion has already been proposed by Gilbert (1941a), who stated that A. *agglutinata* was frequently applied to specimens of *Agaricus volvatus* Pk.

2. *Amanita albocreata* (Atk.) Gilbert. 1941. Inconogr. Mycol. 27(2): 259.

≡ *Amanitopsis albocreata* Atk. 1902. Jour. Myc. 8: 111-112.
≡ *Vaginata albocreata* (Atk.) Murr. 1913. Mycologia 5: 84.

Lectotype (des. mihi): New York - Beebe Lake Woods, 12. vii. 1902, H. H. Whetzel 9822 (CUP) [!].

Fruit bodies small to medium, usually slender, solitary to subgregarious. Pileus 2.5-8 cm diam, convex to expanded, moderately striate or slightly tuberculate-striate, white or with pale maize yellow "R" disc, rarely entirely maize yellow, viscid when moist, glabrous, flesh thin, white; volval remnants as pyramidal warts and/or thin, randomly distributed, floccose patches, easily removed, becoming more firmly attached upon drying. Lamellae crowded, free to narrowly adnexed, rounded toward margin, narrowed at stipe, moderately broad, white, edges often floccose; lamellulae truncate. Stipe 5-15 x 0.5-1.3 cm, tapering slightly stuffed, minutely floccose-scaly; basal bulb abrupt, subglobose to ovoid, white; volva ocreate, sometimes with slight, free margin, or with occasional floccose ringlets or patches near stipe base; exannulate.

Hyphae of pileipellis 2-8 μ diam, interwoven, slightly to strongly gelatinized, hyaline to slightly yellowish in alkaline solution. Lamellar trama bilateral; filamentous hyphae 2-8 μ diam, moderately branched, rarely clamped; inflated cells 20 x 110 μ, clavate to irregularly elongate, terminal or short, terminal chains; subhymenium ramose, hyphae rarely clamped, basidia 35-50 x 4.5-11 μ, 4-sterigmate, rarely clamped. Remnants of volva on pileus a dense to loose tissue of irregularly disposed to apico-basal, terminal chains of inflated cells and single, terminal cells; cells globose, subglobose, broadly elliptic, to ovoid, up to 57 x 83 μ, and elliptic, oblong-elliptic, clavate, astringo-cylindric, cylindric, up to 25 x 125 μ; filamentous hyphae 3-8 μ diam, moderately branched, moderately abundant, rarely clamped, often with conspicuous gloeoplerous segments: volval material at stipe base usually quite similar to that on pileus, but often with a greater proportion of filamentous hyphae. Stipe trama filamentous hyphae 2-8 μ diam, sparsely to moderately branched, often relatively inconspicuous, rarely clamped; inflated cells up to 38 x 286 μ, clavate to elliptic, terminal, longitudinally oriented.

Spores 6.3-8.7 x (7.0)7.9-9.4 μ ($\underline{E}$ = 1.0-1.38; $\underline{E}^m$ = 1.10), globose to broadly elliptic, often adaxially flattened, thin walled, hyaline, spore print color white, nonamyloid; contents guttulate to subgranular; apiculus sublateral, cylindric to occasionally truncate-conic.

Habitat and distribution: Terrestrial in coniferous and deciduous forests, occasionally in open, grassy areas, New York and possibly surrounding states.

Collections examined:

United States:
New York - Beebe Lake Woods, 12. vii. 1902, H. Whetzel 9822 (CUP); West shore Cayuga Lake, 14. vii. 1902, Miss A. T. Young 9757 (CUP); Cayuga Lake Basin, 16. vii. 1902, Miss A. T. Young 13288 (CUP); N. Beebe Lake, 5. viii. 1902, Miss A. T. Young 13306 (CUP); Beebe Lake Woods, 19. vii. 1902, W. Bradfield 9825 (CUP); Enfield Gorge, 25. vii. 1901, J. M. Vann Hook 7062 (CUP).

Nomenclature: The combination *Amanita albocreata* (Atk.) Gilb. is to be considered as validity published. Although Gilbert did not formally make the proposal, he did fulfill the requirements for valid publication (Lanjouw, 1966; Art. 32).

Observations: In his original description of *Amanitopsis albocreata* (1902) Atkinson stated that *Agaricus nivalis* Pk. was probably identical with *A. albocreata*. I feel that this opinion was based only on the similarities of the white pileus and exannulate condition. Examination of type specimens of these two taxa has led me to dispute this synonmy. The spores of *A. albocreata* are globose with an $\underline{E}^m$ value not exceeding 1.08. Although Peck described the spores of Agaricus nivalis as globose, I have found them to be consistently broadly elliptic to elliptic with the $\underline{E}^m$ value not less than 1.2. In addition, the volva of A. albocreata is ocreate, usually with a distinct, free limb, and with irregular ringlets of volval material also found on the lower stipe. Agaricus nivalis, however, has a much more fragile volva, usually breaking up in fragments, but not ocreate.

I feel that A. albocreata is possibly more closely related to A. pantherina through similar volva types. The difference in spore shape, the absence of an annulus, and pileus color separate these two taxa.

3. Amanita crenulata Pk. 1900. Bull. Torr. Bot. Club 27: 15.
 ≡ Venearius crenulatus (Pk.) Murr. 1913. Mycologia 5: 77.
 Lectotype (des. mihi): Massachusetts - Near Boston, 1899, Mrs. E. Blackford s.n.(NYS) [!].

Fruit bodies small to medium slender, solitary to subgregarious. Pileus 2.5-5.5 cm diam, broadly ovate, becoming convex or nearly plane, margin striate, whitish or grayish, sometimes tinged with yellow, viscid, glabrous; volval remnants as thin, whitish, floccose warts or patches, delicate and relatively easily removed, randomly scattered, or as a thin, nearly continuous floccose layer. Lamellae white, free or just reaching stipe, sometimes with a decurrent, pulverulent line, crowded, broadest near the margin of pileus, edges floccose-crenulate; lamellulae truncate. Stipe 2.5-7 x 0.4-0.9 cm, equal or tapering slightly upward, white, stuffed or hollow, floccose mealy above, less so below, basal bulb globose to ovoid, 1-2 cm, white to pallid; volva, if present, as very slight flocculent-mealy material at apex of bulb, usually lacking. Annulus evanescent, found more often in young specimens, rarely in mature specimens.

Hyphae of pileipellis 2-7 µ diam, interwoven to subradial, slightly to strongly gelatinized. Lamellar trama bilateral; hyphae 3-7 µ diam, moderately branched, rarely clamped; inflated cells broadly clavate, terminal or short, terminal chains; subhymenium ramose, clamps not observed. Remnants of volva on pileus a loose tissue of irregularly disposed, short, terminal chains of inflated cells and single, terminal cells; cells elliptic, oblong-elliptic, fusiform, to clavate, up to 51 x 83 µ, and broadly elliptic, ovoid, and subglobose, up to 51 x 70 µ, with subtending cells of chains elongate; filamentous hyphae 2-8 μ diam, moderately abundant, sparsely to moderately branched, clamps not observed: volval material at stipe base usually about equal numbers of inflated cells and hyphae, cells mostly ovoid, broadly elliptic, elliptic, oblong-elliptic, clavate, up to 51 x 95 μ, with lesser numbers of globose and subglobose, usually as short, terminal chains, randomly arranged. Stipe trama hyphae 3-8 μ diam, sparsely to moderately branched, clamps not observed; inflated cells up to 51 x 350 μ, clavate, terminal, longitudinally oriented. Partial veil almost exclusively hyphae, 3-7 μ diam, moderately branched, clamps not observed; inflated cells sparse, only as small, inflated hyphal tips, up to 12 x 38 μ.

Spores 6.3-8.7(11.7) x 7.9-9.4(12.6) μ, ($\underline{E}$ = 1.00-1.29; $\underline{E}^m$ = 1.09), globose to broadly elliptic, often adaxially flattened, thin walled, hyaline, nonamyloid; contents guttulate; apiculus sublateral, cylindric to truncate-conic.

Habitat and distribution: Terrestrial, in mixed forests, Massachusetts and possibly surrounding states.

Collections examined:

United States:
Massachusetts - Near Boston, 1899, Mrs. E. Blackford, s.n.(NYS); Near Boston, 1900, Webster, s.n.(NYS); 10. x. 1902, G. E. Morris, s.n.(NYS).

Observations: This taxon has been frequently synonymized with A. gemmata (Coker, 1917; Gilbert, 1941a). Gilbert synonymized so many taxa with A. gemmata that he produced an extremely broad species concept. Within this pool of characters I feel that several taxa can be distinctly delimited. Amanita crenulata is one of these. It is characterized primarily by the mealy-pulverulent volva at the base, usually missing in mature specimens, as well as globose to subglobose spores. Although only a few collections were available for examinations, these definitive characters were consistent.

In the original description Peck mentioned that specimens of this taxon had been eaten without harm and with excellent flavor. Some recent reports have indicated, however, that a mushroom cautiously identified as A. crenulata (Buck, 1965, 19

69) has caused several cases of intoxication. Further taxonomic examination will be necessary, however, for a confirmation of the identification.

4. *Amanita farinosa* Schw. 1822. Schr. Nat. Ges. Leipzig 1: 79.
 ≡ *Agaricus farinosus* Schw. 1834. Trans. Amer. Phil. Soc. 4: 145.
 ≡ *Amanitopsis farinosus* (Schw.) Pk. 1896. Ann. Rep. N. Y. St. Mus. 50: 87.
 ≡ *Amanitella farinosa* (schw.) Earle. 1909. Bull. N. Y. Bot. Gdn. 5: 449.
 ≡ *Vaginata farinosa* (Schw.) Murr. 1912. Mycologia 4: 3.

Neotype (des. mihi) (Illust. plates 1, 23): North Carolina-Blowing Rock, Watauga and Caldwell Cos., 19. viii. 1901, G. F. Atkinson 10338(CUP-A) [!].

Fruit bodies small to medium, slender solitary to subgregarious. Pileus 2.5-6.5 cm diam, campanulate to plano-convex to plane, occasionally slightly depressed at center, strongly striate to plicate-striate, whitish-gray but always appearing brownish-gray due to the copious volval material, occasionally becoming pallid on margin when all volval material washed away, not noticeably viscid; volval material as a dense layer of mealy-pulverulent remnants covering most of pileus, occasionally organized into small, angular patches or warts, much denser on disc, less so toward the margin, very easily removed. Lamellae white, unchanging usually free, occasionally narrowly adnexed, moderately close, narrowing toward the stipe, anastomosing slightly at the margin, occasionally more toward the center; lamellulae truncate, often scarce. Stipe 3-6.5 x 0.3-0.9 cm, nearly equal, but often tapering downward, stuffed, livid to dirty cream to occasionally white, pulverulent-mealy over entire stipe, basal bulb slight, subglobose to occasionally ovoid, white to pallid; volva always as a band of brownish-gray, pulverulent material around the top of the bulb, never as patches or warts. Annulus wanting, but occasionally a denser area of pulverulence at the apex of the stipe.

Hyphae of pileipellis 2-7 µ diam, interwoven to subradial, very slightly gelatinized. Lamellar trama bilateral, hyphae 2-6 µ diam, sparsely to moderately branched, rarely clamped; inflated cells oblong-elliptic to clavate, terminal and short, terminal chains; subhymenial hyphae inflated ramose, rarely clamped; basidia 4-63 x 3.5-10 μ, 4-sterigmate, rarely clamped. Remnants of volva on pileus an extremely loose tissue of irregularly disposed, terminal chains of inflated cells and single, terminal inflated cells; cells globose, subglobose, ovoid, and broadly elliptic, up to 90 x 90 μ, with oblong-elliptic, elliptic, and astringo-cylindric cells, up to 25 x 90 μ; filamentous hyphae inconspicuous, up to 6 μ diam, sparsely to moderately branched, not clamped: volval remnants on the base of the stipe usually very similar to that on pileus, but occasionally having a greater amount of hyphae and elongate cells. Stipe trama hyphae 2-7 μ diam, sparsely to moderately branched, rarely clamped; inflated cells up to 51 x 350 μ, tending to be short and broad, clavate to oblong-elliptic, terminal, longitudinally oriented.

Spores (4.5)5.5-7.9 x 6.3-7.9(9.4) μ, ($\underline{E}$ = 1.0-1.29; $\underline{E}^m$ = 1.21), globose to broadly elliptic, often adaxially flattened, thin walled, hyaline, spore print color white, nonamyloid; contents guttulate to subgranular; apiculus sublateral, cylindric to truncate-conic.

Habitat and distribution: Terrestrial, growing under conifers or mixed hardwoods, also in open grassy areas, early spring to late fall, throughout the range, from the northeast to the southeast, midwest, southwest, northwest United States. Also reported from southeast Asia.

Collections examined:

United States:
Alabama - Childersburg, 10. vii. 76, David T. Jenkins 1239(DTJ);
California - Smith River, 16. xi. 1937, A. H. Smith 8753(FH);
Florida - Magnesia Springs, 27. v. 1938, W. A. Murrill F16284 (FLAS);
North Carolina - Highlands, 6. ix. 1943, W. C. Coker 13580(NCU); Jackson Co., 20. viii. 1936, W. C. Coker 10185(NCU); Blowing Rock, 19. viii. -22. ix. 1901, G. F. Atkinson 10338(CUP-A); Horse Cove, 22. vii. 1956, L. R. Hesler 22331 (TENN); Whiteside Mtn., 16. viii. 1958, L. R. Hesler 23146(TENN); Bear Pen, Highlands, 21. viii. 1972, David T. Jenkins 129(DTJ); Norton Rd., Highlands, 10. vii. 1971, David T. Jenkins 368(DTJ);

Tennessee - Hesler's woods, 9. vi. 1963, L. R. Hesler 25547(TENN); Cades Cove, 13. viii. 1972, David T. Jenkins 250(DTJ); Cades Cove, 7. viii. 1971, David T. Jenkins 340(DTJ); Roaring Fork, 29. viii. 1972, David T. Jenkins 583(DTJ); Cades Cove, 5. vii. 1973, David T. Jenkins 624(DTJ); Unaka Mtns., 29. vi. 1973, David T. Jenkins 619(DTJ); Cades Cove, 23. viii. 1961, L. R. Hesler 24526(TENN); Indian Gap, 8. viii. 1943, L. R. Hesler s.n.(FH); Cosby Creek, Cocke Co., 24. vii. 1970, R. L. Shaffer 6295(MICH); Cosby, 30. vii. 1936, L. R. Hesler and A. J. Sharp s.n.(FH);
Texas - Richards, 6. ix. 1953, H. D. Thiers 1825(HDT);
Virginia - Giles Co., 22. viii. 1946, R. Singer V-52(FH); Blacksburg, 27. vii. - 3. viii. 1904, W. A. Murrill 334(NY).

Observations: This is one of the more distinct taxa within section *Amanita*. It is characterized by having a rather small stature, small, globose to broadly elliptic spores, a plicate-striate pileus margin, being exannulate, and exhibiting a gray-brown to dark gray, pulverulent volva. This volva type is very distinctive, usually covering most of the pileus with a dense layer of material and leaving a dense, pulverulent ring on the top of the basal bulb. This combination of characters makes it very difficult to confuse this taxon with any other taxon found in the field. Earle (1909) thought this species so distinct as to create a new genus, *Amanitella*, using A. *farinosa* as the type species.

Amanita farinosa seems to be found most frequently in the south, although it has been reported from California (Smith and Hesler, 1938). Specimens have been examined from this location and from Texas. I have seen no reports of its occurrence from Europe, but it has been reported from southeast Asia (Imai, 1938).

This species has in common with A. *crenulata*, A. *wellsii*, and A. *parcivolvata* the very delicate or evanescent, basal volva. This character appears to be the result of the relatively small amount of hyphae found in the volva.

5. *Amanita frostiana* (Pk.) Sacc. 1887. Syll. Fung. 5: 14.
≡ *Agaricus muscarius* var. *minor* Pk. 1869. Rep. N. Y. St. Mus. 23: 69. (non *Agaricus muscarius* var. *minor* S. F. Gray. 1821. Nat. Arrang. Brit. Pl. 1: 600).
≡ *Agaricus frostianus* Pk. 1880. Rep. N. Y. St. Mus. 33: 44.

≡ *Venenarius frostianus* (Pk.) Murr. 1913. Mycologia 5: 76.
[= *Agaricus affinis* Frost, in MSS.; ined.]

Neotype (des. mihi) (Illust. plates 2, 24): New York - Croghan, Lewis Co., no date, C. H. Peck s.n.(NYS) [!].

Fruit bodies small to medium, slender, solitary to subgregarious. Pileus 2-6 cm diam, convex to plano-convex to plane, occasionally slightly depressed at center, moderately to strongly striate, bright orange, often fading toward margin, sometimes to yellow, rarely whitish, viscid when moist, glabrous; volval remnants as floccose warts to appressed patches, thinner toward margin, usually yellow, but occasionally whitish, randomly scattered, but often denser toward the center, usually relatively easily removed, flesh relatively thin, tapering toward margin. Lamellae white but usually margined with yellow flocculence, free, crowded; lamellulae truncate. Stipe 4.7 x 0.4-0.9 cm, tapering upward, slightly expanded at apex, white, often yellow, subfibrillose to subfloccose above annulus, stuffed; basal bulb not abrupt, subglobose to ovoid, white to pallid; volva often as a distinct, white, thin, membranous, free collar, which is usually coated with yellow flocculence, as well as on the lower part of the stipe, or as a thick coat of yellow flocculence without a free, membranous margin. Annulus slight, evanescent, usually yellow, pendant, floccose-membranous.

Hyphae of pileipellis 2-9 μ diam, interwoven to subradial, slightly to strongly gelatinous. Lamellar trama bilateral; hyphae 2-8 μ diam, moderately branched, rarely clamped; inflated cells elongate, up to 35 x 140 μ, terminal or short, terminal chains; subhymenial hyphae ramose to inflated ramose, occasionally clamped; basidia 45-55 x 5-11 μ, 4-sterigmate, rarely clamped. Remnants of volva on pileus a loose fairly dense tissue of apico-basal to irregularly disposed short, terminal chains of inflated cells or single, terminal cells; cells ovoid, broadly elliptic to globose or subglobose, up to 57 x 76 μ, with elliptic, oblong-elliptic, clavate, fusiform, and astringo-cylindric, up to 38 x 160 μ; filamentous hyphae 3-8 μ diam, sparsely to moderately abundant, sparsely to moderately branched, occasionally clamped: volval tissue at the base very similar to that of the pileus, but often with a slightly greater proportion of inflated cells. Stipe trama filamentous hyphae 3-6 μ diam, sparsely to moderately branched, infrequently clamped; inflated cells up to 38 x 300 μ, often tending to be short and broad, clavate, terminal, longitudinally oriented. Partial veil primarily filamentous hyphae, 3-8 μ diam, moderately branched, abundantly clamped; inflated cells sparse, up to 20 x 160 μ, clavate to cylindric, terminal.

Spores 7-10.2 x 7-10.2 μ, (E = 1.0-1.1; E^m = 1.01), globose to rarely subglobose, thin walled, hyaline, spore print color white, nonamyloid; contents guttulate; apiculus sublateral, usually cylindric, occasionally truncate-conic.

Habitat and distribution: Terrestrial, occurring in mixed forests, summer and fall, extending from southern Canada and New England to the southeastern states.

Collections examined:

Canada:
Nova Scotia - Kentville, 27. viii. 1953, K. A. Harrison 44444 (DAOM);
Ontario - Cow Island, 8. x. 1950, J. W. Groves 24273(DAOM); Merivale, 22. vii. 1951, J. W. Groves 26722(DAOM).

United States:
New York - Croghan, Lewis Co., no date, C. H. Peck s.n.(NYS); Adirondacks and Gauswood, 7. ix., C. H. Peck s.n.(NYS); Port Jefferson, vii., C. H. Peck s.n.(NYS); Floodwood, viii., C. H. Peck s.n.(NYS); Lake Placid, viii., C. H. Peck s.n.(NYS); Enfield Gorge, 3. viii. 1947, D. E. Stuntz 3041(WASH);
Tennessee - Cades Cove, v. 1955, L. R. Hesler and T. H. Campbell 21667(TENN).

Nomenclature: *Agaricus affinis*, from which Peck obtained his concept of *Agaricus frostianus*, was never published and, therefore, has no validity as a name. Peck (1880) stated that he did not choose to retain the epithet *affinis* because it had been frequently used for other taxa.

Peck altered the rank of this taxon from a variety of A. *muscaria* to a distinct species upon the examination and recognition of a difference in spore shape.

Observations: Accurate identification of *Amanita frostiana* has been a source of great taxonomic confusion. This is due to the presence of certain characters which allows this taxon to be mistaken for several other well known taxa. It was, of course, first described as *Agaricus muscaris* var. *minor* (Peck, 1869) because of its macroscopic resemblance to the members of the *A. muscaria* complex. The reddish-orange to yellowish-orange pileus, floccose volval patches, and occasional floccose, volval rings at the base corresponded well to the general characters of *A. muscaria*. *Amanita frostiana* can be separated from this complex by the combination of globose spores, a consistently smaller size, and the color of the volval remnants. Those *A. muscaria*-like taxa which have similar pileus colors to *A. frostiana* do not usually exhibit the distinctly yellowish volva, but usually one more tannish to whitish. This relationship might be clarified somewhat through toxicological studies of *A. frostiana* to determine the presence or absence of ibotenic acid and muscimol. Thus far these compounds have not been found in this taxon. *Amanita frostiana* has been reported as being poisonous (Coker, 1917). With the common misidentification between *A. frostiana* and small forms of *A. muscaria*, no one can be sure of the toxic properties until the proper studies are undertaken.

An even greater identification problem exists between *A. frostiana* and *A. flavoconia*. Of all the specimens examined in this study that were labeled *A. frostiana* a large majority were instead *A. flavoconia*. This misidentification results from the similarity of macroscopic features, especially the nearly identical pileus color. One of the obvious morphological differences is the marginal striation, *A. frostiana* being striate and *A. flavovonia* not or only faintly striate. Diagnostic separation is as follows: *A. frostiana* produces globose, nonamyloid spores, while *A. flavoconia* produces smaller, elliptic, amyloid spores. A positive distinction between these two is not difficult, but may require the use of a microscope.

6. *Amanita gemmata* (Fr.) Bertillon in Dechambre. 1866. Dict. Encycl. Sci. Medic. I(3): 496.

   ≡ *Agaricus gemmatus* Fr. 1838. Epicr. Myc.: 12.
   ≡ *Venenarius gemmatus* (Fr.) Murr. 1948. Lloydia 11: 102.
   ≡ *Amanitopsis gemmata* (Fr.) Sacc. 1887. Syll. Fung. 5: 25.

= *Agaricus adnatus* Smith apud Saund. et Smith. 1871. Myc. Ills.: Pl. 20.

≡ *Amanitopsis adnatus* (Smith apud Saund. et Smith) Sacc. 1887. Syll. Fung. 5: 24.

≡ *Pseudofarinaceus adnatus* (Smith apud Saund. et Smith) Kuntze. 1891. Rev. Gen. Plant. 2: 868.

≡ *Vaginata adnata* (Smith apud Saund. et Smith) Kuntze. 1898. Rev. Gen. Plant. 3(2): 539.

= *Amanita junquillea* Quel. 1876. Bull. Soc. Bot. France 23: 324, pl. 3, fig. 10.

≡ *Venenarius junquilleus* (Quel.) Murr. 1913. Mycologia 5: 80.

= *Agaricus russuloides* Pk. 1873. Bull. Buff. Soc. Nat. Sci. 1: 41 [!].

≡ *Amanita russuloides* (Pk.) Sacc. 1887. Syll. Fung. 5: 13.

≡ *Venenarius russuloides* (Pk.) Murr. 1913. Mycologia 5: 77.

= *Amanita junquillea* var. *exannulata* Lange. 1935. Fl. Ag. Dan. 1: 14.

= *Amanita frostiana* var. *pallidipes* Pk. 1899. Rep. N. Y. St. Mus.: 855 [!].

= *Agaricus nivalis* Pk. 1909. N. Y. St. Mus. Bull. 131: 63 [!].

≡ *Agaricus nivalis* Grev. sensu Pk. 1880. Rep. N. Y. St. Mus. 33: 48.

(non *Amanita nivalis* Grev. 1823. Crypt. Scot. 1: 18-19).

= *Agaricus luteus* Oth. apud Trog. 1857. Mitt. Natur. Ges. Bern.: 27.

= *Amanita citrina* Gonn. & Rab. 1869. Myc. Eur.: 2, t.4.

= *Amanita vernalis* Gill. 1884. Tabl. anal.: 6.

[= *Hypophyllum nitido-guttatum* Paul. 1778. Soc. Med.: pl. 15, fig. 3, deval. name].

Type (Illust. plates 3,25): There is no known type specimen for this species. A neotype should be selected from material from France or Sweden.

Fruit bodies small to medium, usually slender, solitary to subgregarious. Pileus 2.5-11 cm diam, hemispherical to convex becoming plano-convex to plane, occasionally with margin slightly reflexed, margin striate, frequently tuberculate-striate, pale yellow "M", buff yellow "R", to wax yellow "M", to amber yellow "M", usually slightly darker on disc, lighter or occasionally becoming whitish on margin, viscid when moist, often strongly so, glabrous, flesh thin, tapering toward margin, white with occasional yellow tint just under pileipellis, not changing color on bruising; volval remnants as angular, floccose patches or small warts, easily removed, occasionally as thin, floccose-membranous patches which cover a large portion of pileus surface, white to dirty-white or pale cream, randomly arranged, frequently dense at center. Lamellae white or very pale cream, usually free but often connected to stipe by floccose line, occasionally slightly adnexed, crowded, broadest toward margin, narrowing toward stipe, edges often floccose; lamellulae truncate. Stipe 4-12(15) x 0.5-1.9 cm, usually tapering upward, with apex slightly expanded, white to pale cream, loosely stuffed to hollow, apex lightly floccose-scaly toward base, occasionally nearly glabrous; basal bulb subglobose, ovoid, clavate, or rarely subradicate, white to pallid; volva as easily removable or subappressed, floccose patches, white to occasionally creamy-tan, on upper bulb and not infrequently on lower part of stem, occasionally as irregular ringlets, or if as a more adnate, free margin, then with floccose material also present. Annulus present or absent, if present usually superior to median, occasionally basal, white with occasional yellowish tint, upper surface floccose-striate, edges occasionally slightly thickened, pendant.

Hyphae of pileipellis 2-8 µ diam, interwoven to subradial, slightly to strongly gelatinized, hyaline to slightly yellowish in alkaline solution. Lamellar trama bilateral; filamentous hyphae 2-8 µ diam, moderately branched and occasionally clamped; inflated cells usually elongate, up to 170 µ long, terminal or in short, terminal chains; subhymenium ramose to slightly inflated-ramose, hyphae rarely clamped; basidia 45-60 x 4-11 µ, 4-sterigmate, rarely clamped. Remnants of volva on pileus a loose to fairly dense tissue of irregularly disposed to apico-basal terminal chains of cells or single, inflated cells; cells of terminal chains mostly broadly elliptic, ovoid, oblong-elliptic, up to 70 x 90 µ, with lesser numbers of globose to subglobose and clavate, fusiform, and cylindric, up to 32 x 127 µ; filamentous hyphae 2-8 µ diam, sparsely to moderately branched, rarely clamped, abundant: volval material at base of stipe very similar to that on pileus. Stipe trama hyphae 2-9 µ diam, sparsely to moderately branched, rarely clamped; inflated cells up to 30 x 320 µ, clavate to elliptic, terminal, longitudinally oriented. Hyphae of partial veil 3-9 µ diam, moderately branched, rarely clamped, with occasional elliptic, clavate, or cylindric, terminal, inflated cells, up to 30 x 140 µ.

Spores (5.5)6.3-7.9(8.5) x (8.7)9.4-10.2(11.0) µ, (E = 1.19-1.57; E^m = 1.39), broadly elliptic to elliptic, often ad-axially flattened, thin walled, hyaline, nonamyloid; contents guttulate to subgranular; apiculus sublateral, cylindric to truncate-conic.

Habitat and distribution: Terrestrial, under conifers and deciduous trees, spring through late fall, found throughout most of the United States, Canada, and Europe.

Collections examined:

Canada:
British Columbia - 4. ix. 1962, R. J. Bandoni, (as Amanita junquillea), 2668(UBC); Vancouver, 21. ix. 1960, F. Waugh, (as Amanita junquillea), s.n.(UBC);
Ontario - 14. vii. 1935, H. T. Gussow, F. Thatcher, M. Timonin, Shiela Thomson F15581(DAOM).

United States:
Alabama - Shades Crest Dr., Birmingham, 17. vii. 75, David T. Jenkins 824(DTJ); Mountain Brook, 31. vii. 75, David T. Jenkins 860 (DTJ); Greentree Apts., Birmingham, 7. ix. 76, Jeannie, Tiffan, and David T. Jenkins 1237(DTJ); Mountain Brook, 8. ix. 76, David T. Jenkins and Mary Ellen MacDonald 1295(DTJ);
California - Mendocino Co., 5. xi. 1964, H. D. Thiers and Gary Breckon 255(HDT); Napa Valley State Park, 10. xii. 1966, Joe Ammirati and Gary Breckon 661(HDT); Mendocino Co., 20. xi. 1965, Gary Breckon 276(HDT); Humboldt Co., 9. x. 1966, Wicklaw, Thiers, Sundberg, Torbbet, and Breckon 536(HDT);
Massachusetts - Walden Pond, vii. 1948, R. Singer (FH); Barre, 23. vii. 1966, J. W. Groves, (as Amanita junquillea), 144798(DAOM); South Acton, 20. viii. 1908, G. E. Morris, (as Amanita russuloides), s.n.(NYS);
Michigan - 13. viii. 1942, A. H. Smith 18521(MICH);
New Jersey - Trenton, 1900, E. B. Sterling, (as Amanita russuloides), s.n.(NYS);
New York - Greenbush, Rensselaer Co., no date, C. H. Peck, holo-

type, (as *Amanita russuloides*), s.n.(NYS); Petersburgh, no date, C. H. Peck, (as *Amanitopsis nivalis*), s.n.(NYS); Worcester, Otsego Co., C. H. Peck, Type, (as *Agaricus nivalis*), s.n.(NYS); North Carolina - Highlands, 20. viii. 1942, 13017(NCU); Ohio - vi. 1907, H. C. Beardslee, s.n.(NYS); Tennessee - Rich Mtn., Blount Co., 24. vi. 1934, L. R. Hesler 4222(TENN); Knoxville, 13. vii. 1943, L. R. Hesler and A. H. Smith 15762(TENN); Island Home, Knox Co., 22, vi. 1934, L. R. Hesler 4221(TENN); Jamestown, Fentress Co., 8. vii. 1934, L. R. Hesler 4225(TENN); Blount Co., 23. viii. 1934, L. R. Hesler 6262 (TENN); Knoxville, 24. vii. 1936, L. R. Hesler 8964(TENN); Near laboratory, 15. vii. 1955, L. R. Hesler 21861(TENN); Riverbend, Knox Co., 17. x. 1962, L. R. Hesler 24970(TENN); Cades Cove, GSMNP, 15. viii. 1963, L. R. Hesler 26109(TENN); Cades Cove, GSMNP, 3. ix. 1965, R. H. Petersen and L. R. Hesler 28212(TENN); Cades Cove, GSMNP, 28. vi. 1967, L. R. Hesler 29719(TENN); Roaring Fork, GSMNP, 24. viii. 1972, David T. Jenkins 46(DTJ); Cades Cove, GSMNP, no date, David T. Jenkins, 177(DTJ); Colonial Golf Course, Knoxville, 29. vi. 1971, David T. Jenkins 243(DTJ); Parsons Branch, GSMNP, no date, David T. Jenkins 251(DTJ); Fairfield Glade Resort, 19. vii. 1972, David T. Jenkins 542(DTJ); Cades Cove, GSMNP, 25. vii. 1972, David T. Jenkins 549(DTJ); West High School, Knoxville, 14. viii. 1972, David T. Jenkins 566(DTJ).

Extra-limital:

Czechoslovakia:
Fritzens, 19. x. 1952, M. Moser 25070(TENN).
France:
Montmorence, 1910, E. Boudier, (as *Amanita junquillea*), 24561 (CUP); Louvaine, v. 1909, M. Boue, (as *Amanita junquillea*), s.n. (P); Pontarlier, 23. vii. 1910, G. F. Atkinson and E. Boudier, (as *Amanita junquillea*), 24717(CUP); Raon L'Etape, 17. viii. 1910, G. F. Atkinson and R. Maire, (as *Amanita junquillea*), 24952(CUP); no date, M. Boue, s.n.(P).
Holland: Leiden, x. 1912, Van der Lerk s.n.(L); Prov. Guid-Holland, 9. xi. 1951, Bas 24454(TENN).
Italy:
Appiano, vi. 1926, G. Bresadola s.n.(BPI).

Fries's original description of the pileus color of A. *gemmata as* "colore A. *muscarii*" has created a topic for nomenclatural discussion. The concept of A. *gemmata* used by modern mycologists includes a pale yellow to orange-yellow cap, not red, orange, or white, colors given to A. *muscarius* in the same publication. This confusion originated from the plates by Paulet of *Hypophyllum nitido-guttatum*, from which Fries obtained his concept of *Agaricus gemmatus*, which was published twice (1778, 1855). The plate in the first publication, according to Maire (1913), showed the mushroom as having a "citrine-doree" cap, while the plate in the second publication shows a fruit body with an orange to red pileus. Fries evidently saw the first plate, since he published *Agaricus gemmatus* before the second plate was published, but his comparison of A. *gemmatus* to the colors of A. *muscarius* has produced some unnecessary confusion.

Observations: *Amanita gemmata* is one of the better known names in section *Amanita*, yet is is probably one of the more confused taxa. Because of the golden yellow to pale yellow to whitish color of the pileus, a wide variety of light colored fruit bodies, including faded forms of more distinctly colored taxa, have been identified as A. *gemmata* (Gilbert, 1941a).

Without doubt, there is significant variation within this taxon. This is not infrequent in taxa found world wide in distribution. As previously stated Gilbert placed many names in synonymy with A. *gemmata*. Several of these I have determined to be separate taxa, at both the species and infraspecific levels. *Amanita albocreata* and A. *crenulata* have been retained as separate species while A. *chrysoblema* has been synonymized with A. *muscaria* var. *alba*, A. *praegemmata* has been synonymized with A. *pantherina* var. *pantherinoides*, and A. *velatipes* has been made a vareity of A. *pantherina*. I feel that the species concept including Gilbert's synonymies was much too broad, creating a taxon which was difficult to define.

Two taxa with white to pale yellow pilei have also been synonymized with A. *gemmata*. Gilbert (1941a) has already recognized the synonymy of A. *nivalis* Pk. based on similar spore size and the appressed, floccose volva at the base. For very similar reasons I have found A. *frostiana* var. *pallidipes* to be a synonym of A. *gemmata*. This taxon is not a form of A. *frostiana* because of elliptic spores, those of A. *frostiana* being globose.

The above taxonomic description of A. *gemmata* is proposed in an attempt to stabilize the identification of members of this taxon in North America. It is well understood that further examination of specimens from other areas of the world may alter this concept somewhat. I have examined European specimens, most of which conformed to the above description. There were several specimens, however, which were quite variable and could not be identified at this time.

The question of toxicity of A. *gemmata* has long been a point of concern. A study by Benedict, Tyler, and Brady (1966) showed that their specimens of A. *gemmata* contained no ibotenic acid or muscimol, which are the toxic substances found in A. *pantherina* and A. *muscaria* specimens. Color varieties which were thought to be hybrids between A. *gemmata* and A. *pantherina* were found to contain gradient quantities of the above toxins. A recent study by Chilton and Ott, (1976), however, resulted in the detection of small amounts of ibotenic and muscimol in an A. *gemmata* specimen from Washington state.

7. Amanita *monticulosa* (Berk. & Curt.) Sacc. 1887. Syll. Fung. 5: 18.

≡ *Agaricus monticulosus* Berk. & Curt. 1853. Ann. Nat. Hist. 12(2): 418.

Holotype: South Carolina - ix., M. A. Curtis 2853, sheet II, packet II, right-hand fruit body, (K) [!].

Fruit bodies small to medium, slender, solitary. Pileus 5-8 cm diam, convex to plano-convex, with occasional slight umbo, areolate, margin not or faintly striate, slightly viscid when moist, flesh thin, tapering toward margin; volval remnants as angular, pyramidal, or truncate warts in the center of each areola, becoming more flocculent toward margin of pileus. Lamellae free, ventricose, remote, forming a well defined gap around the apex of the stipe. Stipe 3-6 x 0.4-0.8 cm, slightly tapering upward, white, stuffed to hollow, fibrillose, basal bulb subglobose to ovoid; volva scaly to felted-subfloccose patches at apex of bulb. Annulus thick, distant, floccose.

Hyphae of pileipellis 2-7 µ diam, interwoven, slightly gelatinized. Lamellar trama bilateral, with significant number of gloeoplerous hyphae; basidia up to 47 x 4-11 µ. Remnants of volva on pileus a loose to moderately dense tissue of apico-basal to occasionally irregularly disposed, terminal chains of inflated cells and single, terminal cells; cells globose, subglobose, to broadly elliptic, up to 38 x 51 μ, with elliptic, oblong-elliptic, to clavate cells, up to 20 x 76 μ; gloeoplerous hyphae abundant, very sparsely branched, up to 15 μ diam, with remaining hyphae 3-8 μ diam, moderately branched: volva tissue at the base very similar to that on pileus with a very slight increase in the number of inflated cells. Stipe trama composed of elongate cells and undifferentiated, filamentous hyphae.

Spores 7-8(9) x 10-11.2(12.5) μ, (E = 1.19-1.50; E^m = 1.35), broadly elliptic to elliptic, often adaxially flattened, thin walled, smooth, hyaline, nonamyloid; contents guttulate to subgranular; apiculus sublateral.

Habitat and distribution: Terrestrial, moist, sandy woods, South Carolina and possibly other nearby southeastern states.

Collections examined:

United States:
South Carolina - M. A. Curtis 2853(K).

Nomenclature: For lectotypification see type studies.

Observations: It is very difficult at this time to speculate as to a possible relationship of A. *monticulosa* with other taxa in this section. Singer (1955) indicated a relationship with the A. "*muscaria-cothurnata*" complex. The lack of a well defined, free margined volva separates it from A. *pantherina* var. *multisquamosa* (= A. *cothurnata*). The disposition of the floccose material on the basal bulb and the spore size could indicate a possible relationship with the A. *muscaria* complex, although this evidence is not conclusive. The abundance of gloeoplerous hyphae and the areolate pileus seem to separate A. *monticulosa* from most taxa, although a few specimens within the A. *muscaria* complex frequently have significant numbers of gloeoplerous hyphae in the volva. *Amanita agglutinata* has an abundance of this type of hyphae, but is separated by its lobed, free-margined volva and its elongate spores.

8. *Amanita muscaria* (L. per Fr.) Hooker. 1821. Flora Scotica 2: 19.

A number of varieties and forms of *A. muscaria* have been reported to occur in the United States. Included within this group are *A. muscaria* var. *muscaria*, var. *formosa*, var. *alba*, var. *regalis*, f.s. *americana*, f. *umbrina*, and subsp. *flavivolvata*. During this study representatives of all of these taxa were examined microscopically and were found to be quite similar. Several morphological differences have been noted, both from fresh specimens and notes accompanying herbarium specimens, the most obvious being coloration. As in past taxonomic treatments, therefore, the color of the pileus, volva, annulus, gills, and stipe appears to remain as one of the most important, definitive, infraspecific characters for this group.

Because the identification of these taxa is based partially upon the color of certain structures, the lack of accurate color notes accompanying herbarium specimens hampered this study somewhat. Therefore, I have been able to include only five specific taxa with this complex. I have defined and described only those taxa that I have personally collected or that were described by complete and reliable notes. These five taxa include *A. muscaria* var. *muscaria*, var. *formosa*, var. *alba*, var. *flavivolvata*, and a new variety, *persicina*.

Two taxa which have brown pieli, var. *regalis* and f. *umbrina*, have been reported only from the western states. Variety *regalis* is described as exhibiting a more hepatic color on the pileus and a yellowish volva, while in f. *umbrina* the pileus is more umber with whitish volval remnants. Because the pileus colors come very close to those of *A. pantherina*, which is morphologically similar to members of the *A. muscaria* complex, judgment on these taxa will be reserved until I can see them in the fresh condition.

The fate of f.s. *americana* is discussed under var. *persicina*.

8a. *Amanita muscaria* var. *muscaria* (L. per Fr.) Hooker. 1821. Flora Scotica 2: 19.

≡ *Agaricus muscarius* (L.) Fr. 1821. Syst. Mycol. 1: 16.

[≡ *Agaricus muscarius* L. 1753. Species Plant. 2: 1172; deval. name].

[≡ *Agaricus caulescens* lamellis dimidiatis solitariis; stipite volvato, apice dilatato, basi ovato Linnaeus. 1745. Flora Suecica p. 379, no. 1076 (referred to by fires as "Flora Suecica 1235")].

[≡ *Agaricus caulescens*, petiolo albo et basim globose, pileo sanguineo, verrucis et lamella albis Linnaeus. 1737. Flora Lapponica, no. 515; nom. illeg.]. [This fungus is surely cited in "Species Plantarum" although with its polynomial slightly changed and with the wrong number (595) instead of 515): referred to in "Flora Suecica" correctly].

≡ *Venenarius muscarius* (Linnaeus per Fries) Earle. 1909. Bull. N. Y. Bot. Gard. 5: 450.

[≡ *Hypophyllum muscarium* (Linn.) Paulet. 1778. Soc. Med. t. 11, f. 2-3; deval. name].

[≡ *Agaricus imperialis* Batsch. 1783. Elench. Fung.: 56; deval. name].

[≡ *Agaricus nobilis* Bolt. 1788. Hist. Fung. 1: 46; deval name].

[≡ *Agaricus pseudo-aurantiacus* Bull. 1809. Hist. Champ. 2: 673; deval name].

Neotype (Illust. plates 4, 26), (Jenkins & Petersen, 1976): Angermanland: Nordingra Parish, Sweden. Summer, 1974, coll. R. H. Petersen, TENN 39847.

Fruit bodies small to large, solitary to subgregarious. Pileus 5-25 cm diam, convex to plano-convex to plano-depressed, faintly to strongly striate, sometimes slightly appendiculate, blood-red to red-orange, darker at center, becoming lighter toward margin, viscid, glabrous, flesh white, but yellow under pileipellis; volval remnants as whitish, floccose warts or patches, arranged randomly to nearly in concentric rings, often passing into thin, floccose material at margin. Lamellae crowded to moderately crowded, free to adnexed or just touching stipe, broad to moderately broad, white to whitish, often with minutely floccose edges; lamellulae abruptly to rounded truncate. Stipe 5-18 x 0.3-3 cm, tapering upward with apex expanded, stuffed to hollow, white to cream-white, fibrous to floccose-fibrillose-scaly; basal bulb subglobose, ovoid, clavate, to subradicate, whitish to pallid; volva irregular, ascending rings of small to medium floccose warts or patches, often with a shallow rim on upper portion of bulb, lower part of stipe often having several floccose, warty or recurved, scaly ascending rings. Annulus apical to subapical,

membranous to submembranous-felted, pendant, fragile, striate
above, floccose below, edge often with small to medium floccose
chunks of volval material, often collapsing.

Hyphae of pileipellis 3-10 µ diam, interwoven to subradial,
slightly to strongly gelatinized, hyaline to slightly yellowish
in alkaline solution. Lamellar trama bilateral; filamentous
hyphae 2-9 µ diam, moderately branched, rarely clamped; inflated
cells elongate, terminal, or in short, terminal chains; subhymenium ramose to slightly inflated-ramose, hyphae rarely clamped;
basidia 40-63 x 3.5-11 µ, 4-sterigmate, occasionally clamped.
Remnants of volva on pileus a dense to loose tissue of irregularly disposed and apico-basal, terminal chains of inflated
cells and single, terminal cells; cells globose, subglobose,
broadly elliptic, ovoid, elliptic, oblong-elliptic, fusiform
clavate, to astringo-cylindric, up to 76 x 130 µ; filamentous
hyphae 3-10 µ diam, abundant, moderately branched, clamped,
occasionally with conspicuous gloeoplerous segments: volval
material at base of stipe very similar to that on pileus, often
with a greater ratio of filamentous hyphae than on pileus.
Stipe trama filamentous hyphae 2-8 µ diam, sparsely branched,
usually clamped; inflated cells up to 40 x 380 µ, clavate, terminal, longitudinally oriented. Partial veil composed primarily
of moderately branched, clamped, filamentous hyphae, 3-9 µ diam,
with medium sized, terminal, clavate to cylindric, inflated
cells.

Spores (6.3)7-8.7 x 9.4-11(13) µ, ($\underline{E}$ = 1.19-1.67; $\underline{E}^m$ = 1.40),
broadly elliptic to elongate, adaxially flattened, thin walled,
hyaline, spore print color white to pale cream nonamyloid; contents guttulate to subgranular; apiculus sublateral, cylindric to
truncate-conic.

<u>Habitat and distribution</u>: Terrestrial, under coniferous
and deciduous trees, not uncommon in western states, much rarer in
the eastern states, also Canada and Europe.

<u>Collections examined</u>:

Canada:
<u>British Columbia</u> - Mt. Seymour, 25. x. 1965, L. Broome s.n.(UBC);
Vancouver, 28. ix. 1960, Joyce Lamko s.n.(UBC).

United States:

California - Humboldt Co., 22. xi. 1969, H. D. Thiers 24384(HDT);
Mendocino Co., 18. xi. 1961, H. D. Thiers 8879(HDT);
Connecticut - Storrs, 12. ix. 1912, C. Thom s.n.(BPI);
Maine - Bar Harbor, x. 1935, E. E. Morse s.n.(FH);
Michigan - Oakland Co., 8. x. 1937, A. H. Smith s.n.(MICH);
New York - 19. ix. 1911, B. B. Higgins 23201(CUP); Albany Co., 29. ix. 1969, S. Smith and D. Moore 44982(NYS);
Oregon - 15. x. 1944, A. H. Smith 19750(MICH);
Washington - Lonmire, 27. ix. 1932, G. Flett s.n.(FH).

Extra-limital:

Belgium:
Liege, 23. x. 1972, David T. Jenkins 753(DTJ).
Germany:
Berlin, Exs. Sydow., Mycoth. Mar. no. 618, (S).
Holland:
Noord Brabant, 3, xi. 1951, C. Bas 97(L); 12. ix. 1953, C. Bas (L).
Sweden:
Upsala, Fungi Exs. Suecici no. 1, 26. viii. 1933, S. Lundell (S); approx. 1770, Montin s.n.(S).

Observations: The typical, blood-red form of A. *muscaria* is one of the most distinctive taxa in section *Amanita*. Unless encountering an aberrant form, almost no mycologist should have any difficulty in identifying this mushroom. The blood-red pileus, white, floccose, volval patches, the ringlets of white, volval tissue on the base, and the white annulus on a white stipe unquestionably separate this mushroom from any other in the section.

Amanita muscaria can be found in many sections of Europe, Asia, and other areas of the world. In the earlier mycological history of the United States it was not thought to occur in this country as the bright red form. The more common form found was red on the disc but orange toward the margin. As mycological interest became greater the true form was found to occur quite frequently in the western states and occasionally in the eastern states (Zeller, 1933; Seaver and Shope, 1935; Hotson, 1936). Its occurrence in the southeastern states is questionable, with other color forms apparently replacing it. I have had personal reports that it does occur along the gulf coast during good, rainy seasons, but I have not yet observed this first hand.

This variety of A. *muscaria* is well known from its morphological characters, but has gained an equal recognition based on its toxicity and psychotomimetic properties. As early as the thirteenth century it was known to kill flies (Tyler, 1958). It was reported in the eighteenth century that certain tribes in Siberia used the mushroom as an hallucinogen. This stimulated research in many parts of the world in an attempt to isolate the active substance. Substances were later isolated several times, but were not identified until Takemoto et al. (1964) and Eugster et al. identified ibotenic acid and muscimol respectively.

8b. *Amanita muscaria* var. *alba* Peck. 1893. Rep. N. Y. St. Mus. 46: 133.

≡ *Agaricus muscarius* var. *albus* Peck. 1880. Rep. N. Y. St. Mus. 33: 44.

= *Amanita chrysoblema* Atk. in Kauff. 1918. The Agaricaceae of Michigan 1: 613-614 [!].

Neotype (Illust. plate 27) (des. mihi): New York - Albany and Delmar, ix., C. H. Peck s.n.(NYS) [!].

Fruit bodies small to large, usually slender, solitary to subgregarious. Pileus 4-19 cm diam, convex to plano-convex, becoming plane, occasionally with margin slightly raised, faintly striate to tuberculate-striate, white, pallid, silvery white, cream-buff "R", pale pinkish-buff "R", to capucine-buff "R", subviscid, glabrous, flesh white, yellowish underneath pileipellis; volval remnants as thin, relatively small, floccose patches of angular to pyramidal warts, pallid to pale tannish, adhering quite firmly to pileipellis, randomly arranged or more often in near concentric rings, frequently passing into floccose-fibrillose material nearer margin of pileus. Lamellae crowded to moderately crowded, free to narrowly adnexed, broad to moderately broad, white to pale cream, edges often minutely floccose; lamellulae abruptly to rounded truncate. Stipe 5-14 x 0.7-2.2 cm, tapering upward with apex slightly expanded, stuffed, floccose-fibrillose above annulus, becoming fibrous to lacerate below, flesh often turning yellowish upon bruising or cutting; basal bulb subglobose to ovoid to subradicate, white to pallid to pale buff; volva as floccose patches or with occasional, slight rim at apex of bulb, usually with ascending rings of floccose material on lower stipe, pallid to pale tannish. Annulus floccose-striate above, strongly floccose below, pale yellow to cream to pallid, at first pendant but soon collapsing. No distinct smell or taste.

Hyphae of pileipellis 3-10 μ diam, interwoven to subradial, slightly to strongly gelatinized, hyaline to slightly yellowish in alkaline solution. Lamellar trama bilateral; filamentous hyphae moderately branched, clamped; inflated cells elongate, terminal or short, terminal chains; hyphae of subhymenium ramose to slightly inflated, clamped; basidia 47-68 x 4-12.6 μ, 4-sterigmate, occasionally clamped. Remnants of volva on pileus a dense to loose tissue of apico-basal to irregularly disposed, terminal chains of inflated cells and single, terminal cells; cells globose, subglobose, broadly elliptic, ovoid, elliptic, clavate, fusiform, pyriform, up to 74 x 96 μ; filamentous hyphae 3-9 μ diam, abundant, moderately branched, occasionally to abundantly clamped; gloeoplerous hyphae often locally abundant: volval material at base similar to that on pileus but often with higher proportion of filamentous hyphae and elongate cells. Stipe trama filamentous hyphae 2-11 μ diam, sparsely to moderately branched, often relatively inconspicuous, occasionally clamped; inflated cells up to 25 x 400 μ, clavate to elliptic, terminal, longitudinally oriented. Partial veil composed primarily of moderately branched, clamped, filamentous hyphae, 3-8 μ diam; inflated cells 13 x 130 μ, terminal, clavate to cylindric; gloeoplerous hyphae occasional.

Spores (6.3)7-8.7(9.4) x (7.9)9.4-12(14.1) μ, ($\underline{E}$ = 1.19-1.69: $\underline{E}^m$ = 1.41), broadly elliptic to elongate, often adaxially flattened, thin walled, hyaline, spore print color white to pale cream, nonamyloid; contents guttulate to subgranular; apiculus sublateral, cylindric to occasionally truncate-conic.

<u>Habitat</u> <u>and</u> <u>distribution</u>: Terrestrial in coniferous and hardwood forests, western, mid-western and northeastern United States, and southeastern and southwestern Canada.

<u>Collections</u> <u>examined</u>:

Canada:

Quebec - Aylmer, 19. ix. 1965, J. W. Groves and W. G. Dore, (as *Amanita subalpina* Smith in herb.), 110423(DAOM).

United States:

Idaho - McCall, 31. viii. 1964, H. D. Thiers 11537(HDT); McCall, 5. ix. 1964, H. D. Thiers 11681(HDT); Priest River Exp. Forest, 12. viii. 1964, K. A. Harrison, (as *Amanita subalpina* Smith in herb.), 107005(DAOM);

Michigan - Silver Lake, 7. x. 1945, A. H. Smith 21215(MICH); Chelsea, 20. ix. 1907, C. H. Kauffman, (as *Amanita chrysoblema*), s.n. (CUP-A); North of Marquette, 30. viii. 1971, David T. Jenkins 438(DTJ);

New York - Alcove, viii. 1892, C. L. Shear 3(NY); Albany and Delmar, ix., C. H. Peck s.n.(NYS);

Pennsylvania - Bethlehem, ix., W. Harles s.n.(NYS);

Washington - Longmire, 15. ix. 1948, A. H. Smith 31294(MICH).

Nomenclature: For the neotypification of A. *muscaria* var. *alba* see type studies.

Observations: *Amanita muscaria* var. *alba* appears to be a consistent color variety and not the result of the fading of a darker colored specimen. I have collected several specimens in Michigan, all of which had consistently pallid coloration, never with any indication of having previously been a darker color. Even the more immature fruit bodies possessed the white to silver white pileus color. There are several other characters which support this being a separate taxon. The volval remnants of var. *alba* are tannish in color while those of var. *muscaria* are white. The flesh of the stipe in var. *alba* turns a yellowish color upon cutting or bruising, a reaction not found in the red form. The annulus of var. *alba* is usually a creamy yellow to pallid color, while in var. *muscaria* it is white.

Amanita chrysoblema was apparently based on only one or a few collections. Macroscopically and microscopically it is very similar to A. *muscaria* var. *alba*. The pileus is white to cream with floccose patches. An annulus is present which occasionally has yellowish floccules on the surface, also common in var. *alba*, especially upon drying. The stipe is fibrous-scaly to lacerate near the bottom, with the volva often disposed as ringlets on the lower stipe. Finally, the spores fit within the range of var. *alba*.

8c. *Amanita muscaria* var. *formosa* (Pers. per Fr.) Bertillon in DeChambre. 1866. Dict. Encycl. Sci. Med. I(3): 496.

[≡ *Amanita muscaria* var. B (*formosa*) Pers. 1799. Obs. Myc. 2: 27; deval. name].

≡ *Agaricus muscarius* var. *formosa* (Pers.) Fr. 1854. Monogr. Hymen. Sueciae I.: 7.

≡ *Amanita muscaria* f. *formosa* (Pers. per Fr.) Gonn. & Raben. 1869. Myc. Europ.: 5.

Type: (Illust. plate 5, 28), There is no known type specimen for this taxon.

Fruit bodies small to large, usually slender, solitary to subgregarious. Pileus 4.5-17 cm diam, convex to plano-convex becoming plane or with margin slightly raised, striate to tuberculate-striate, primuline yellow "R", to capucine yellow "R", to zinc orange "R", or deep orange, becoming lighter toward margin, slightly viscid, glabrous, flesh yellowish under pileipellis, tapering toward margin of pileus; volval remnants as yellowish to pale buff to tan, floccose patches or irregular warts, densely to completely covering pileus when young, becoming broken into scattered patches with age, varying in size, easily removed, usually becoming more flocculent near the margin. Lamellae white to pale cream, free or connected to stipe by a faint, floccose line, crowded, broadest near the margin, narrowed at the stipe, edges often strongly floccose; lamellulae truncate, fairly numerous. Stipe 4.15 x 0.7-3 cm, equal or tapering upward, slightly expanded at apex, white to cream buff to pale yellow-orange, stuffed, finely floccose-fibrillose above annulus, fibrous, fibrous-scaly, squarrose-scaly to lacerate below, flesh turning yellowish when bruised; basal bulb subglobose to subradicate, 1.0-4.5 x 3.5-7 cm, white to pallid; volva as broken rings of pale yellow to tannish, floccose material on apex of bulb, also on lower stipe, frequently as more lacerate, ascending rings. Annulus superior, frequently evanescent, lightly floccose on top, strongly so underneath, double-edged, pendant, readily adhering to stipe, pinkish-buff "R" to cream-buff "R".

Hyphae of pileipellis 2-9 μ diam, interwoven to subradial,

slightly gelatinized, hyaline to slightly yellowish in alkaline solution. Lamellar trama bilateral; filamentous hyphae 3-9 μ diam, moderately branched, occasionally clamped; inflated cells elongate, terminal or in short, terminal chains; subhymenium ramose, hyphae occasionally clamped; basidia 45-62 x 4.7-12.6 μ, 4-sterigmate, occasionally clamped. Remnants of volva on pileus a loose to fairly dense tissue of irregularly disposed to apico-basal, terminal chains of inflated cells and single, terminal cells; cells globose, subglobose, broadly elliptic, and ovoid, up to 84 x 94 μ, with elliptic, oblong-elliptic, clavate, fusiform, cylindric, up to 36 x 130 μ; filamentous hyphae moderately branched, 3-9 μ diam, abundant, clamped: volval material at base very similar to that on pileus. Stipe trama filamentous hyphae 2-8 μ diam, sparsely to moderately branched, infrequently clamped; inflated cells up to 32 x 381 μ, clavate to fusiform-elliptic, terminal, longitudinally oriented. Partial veil primarily filamentous hyphae, 2-7 μ diam, moderately branched, occasionally clamped; inflated cells sparse, terminal, clavate to cylindric, usually less than 100 μ long.

Spores 6.3-7.9 x (8.7)9.4-11(12.9) μ, ($\underline{E}$ = 1.24-1.54; $\underline{E}^m$ = 1.36), broadly elliptic to elliptic, adaxially flattened, thin walled, hyaline, spore print color white, nonamyloid; contents guttulate to subgranular; apiculus sublateral, cylindric to occasional truncate-conic.

Habitat and distribution: Terrestrial, under coniferous and deciduous trees, usually early to late fall, western, midwestern, and northeastern United States and possibly southern portions of Canada.

Collections examined:

United States:
California - Napa Co., 24. xi. 1963, G. Breckon and H. D. Thiers 10823(HDT); Humboldt Co., 16. x. 1971, H. D. Thiers 28374(HDT);
Massachusetts - x., Webster s.n.(NYS);
Michigan - Marquette, 30. viii. 1971, David T. Jenkins 439(DTJ); Marquette, 2. ix. 1971, David T. Jenkins 453(DTJ);
New York - Schenectady, ix., C. H. Peck s.n.(NYS); Essex Co., 26. ix. 1969, C. T. Rogerson, S. J. Smith, D. Moore s.n.(NYS); Bol-

ton, viii., C. H. Peck s.n.(NYS); Cayuga Lake Basin, 1. x. 1907, Brown 22160(CUP).

Observations: In the northeastern, midwestern, and western United States and portions of Canada there is a variety of A. *muscaria* with a pileus color from primuline yellow "R" to zinc orange "R". This particular form has usually been referred to as A. *muscaria* var. *formosa*. As with some other color varieties of A. *muscaria* there has been much debate as to the validity of this taxon, with some mycologists rejecting var. *formosa* as merely a faded form of the typical red variety. Gilbert (1941a) stated that the mushrooms called var. *formosa* in Europe normally showed a blood red or orange pileipellis, but that they became yellow under the influence of moist humus. It is impossible, of course, to determine whether or not the mushroom described by Persoon (1799)as having a golden yellow pileus with a yellow volva and annulus was the result of discoloration of the typically red variety. This theory becomes even weaker when considering the fact that not only would the pileus color have to change, but also that of the volva and annulus, from white in the red variety to yellowish or tannish in var. *formosa*. Gilbert did recognize, however, that the pileus of the "American var. *formosa*" had a naturally yellow pileus, not the result of fading. I have also found this to be true of the specimens that I have collected. Heim (1965) felt that the color of var. *formosa* was the result of A. *muscaria* (the red variety) being subjected to darkness during its growth in the soil or humus.

As Gilbert intimated above there is speculation that the mushroom called var. *formosa* in the United States is not the same as that found in Europe. Hotson (1936) related the theories of Jakob E. Lange and S. M. Zeller concerning the "American *formosa*". Following a trip to the west coast of the United States in 1931, Dr. Lange (1934) stated that he believed the yellow variety found there to be different from anything found in Europe. He felt that it was identical with the color form found in the eastern United States.

I must agree that the forms in the west and the east are very similar, with slight color variations. After examining specimens from the United States and comparing them with European concepts however, I can find very little difference. The macroscopic features appear to be very similar. The lack of color notes, however, prevented accurate comparison of this character. Of the American specimens I have examined in the fresh condition the volval material varied from yellowish-white to yellowish-tan to tan, with the annulus usually whitish but frequently with a yellowish tint. This does not vary a great deal from those characteristics originally described by Persoon. Until I can observe European material in the fresh condition or obtain reliable color notes, I will continue to refer to this American color variety as A. *muscaria* var. *formosa*.

8d. *Amanita muscaria* var. *flavivolvata* (Singer) Jenkins stat. nov.
Basionym: *Amanita muscaria* subsp. *flavivolvata* Singer. 1958. Sydowia 11: 374.
Holotype: (Illust. plates 6, 13, 14, 18, 19, 29), California-San Francisco, 21. i. 1958, R. Singer N1506(MICH).

Fruit bodies small to large, solitary to subgregarious. Pileus 5-17 cm diam, convex to plano-convex to plano-depressed, faintly striate, orange-red "M" to brownish-red "M" on disc, becoming paler toward margin, viscid, glabrous, flesh white, but brownish-red to yellow under pileipellis; volval remnants as deep yellow "M" to orange-yellow "M", floccose to floccose-fibrillose patches, randomly distributed, often passing into thin, floccose material at margin. Lamellae crowded to moderately crowded, free to approximate, broad to moderately broad, white to pale cream, edges smooth to minutely floccose; lamellulae numerous, truncate. Stipe 7-13.5 x 0.9-2.3 cm, tapering upward slightly or cylindric, slightly expanded at apex, densely stuffed, white to cream, becoming tannish upon handling, fibrous to fibrous-scaly may or may not split into typical, ascending rings on lower portion; basal bulb ovoid, whitish to tannish; volva occasionally as large, irregular warts, in or not in ascending rings, or as irregular flocculence on upper portion of bulb and lower stipe. Annulus superior, submembranous-felted, typical double margin, yellow volval material on underside, evanescent.

Hyphae of pileipellis 2-9 μ diam, interwoven to subradial, slightly to strongly gelatinized, hyaline to slightly yellowish in alkaline solution. Lamellar trama bilateral; filamentous hyphae 3-9 μ diam, moderately branched, clamped; inflated cells elongate, terminal or in short, terminal chains; subhymenium ramose, hyphae clamped; basidia 46-56.8 x 3.9-14.8 μ, 4-sterigmate, clamped. Remnants of volva on pileus a dense to loose tissue of irregularly disposed and apico-basal, terminal chains of inflated cells and single, terminal cells; cells subglobose, broadly elliptic, pyriform, ovoid, up to 65.7 x 65.7 μ, with elliptic, oblong-elliptic, and clavate, up to 25 x 78.3 μ; filamentous hyphae 2-8 μ diam, abundant, moderately branched, clamps rare, gloeoplerous hyphae moderately abundant: volval material at base of stipe very similar to that on pileus, but with cells slightly larger and less gloeoplerous hyphae. Stipe trama filamentous hyphae 2.5-8 μ diam, moderately branched, abundant, and conspicuous, clamps common; inflated cells up to 37.6 x 281.7 μ, clavate, terminal, longitudinally oriented. Upper surface of partial veil mostly filamentous hyphae, sparsely to moderately branched, 2.3-8 μ diam, clamps abundant; inflated cells moderately abundant, oblong-elliptic to clavate, terminal, up to 10.8 x 30.8 μ; lower surface very similar, but with slightly larger cells, up to 31 x 125 μ; not infrequently tissue of the volva will also be found on this lower surface.

Spores 7.0-7.8(8.6) x 10.2-11.7 μ, ($\underline{E}$ - 1.36-1.67; $\underline{E}^m$ = 1.42), broadly elliptic to elongate, adaxially flattened, thin walled, hyaline, nonamyloid, contents guttulate to subgranular; apiculus sublateral, cylindric to truncate-conic.

<u>Habitat</u> <u>and</u> <u>distribution</u>: Terrestrial, under conifers and deciduous, extending from the western states into the southern states and Mexico, and possibly up into the southern Appalachians.

Collections examined:

<u>United States</u>:
<u>Alabama</u> - Dauphin Island, 30. xi. 1976, Paul Johnson 1351(DTJ);
<u>California</u> - San Jose Pacifica, 1, viii. 1976, Steve Pollock 1327 (DTJ);
<u>Colorado</u> - Aspen, 11. viii. 1976, Steve Pollock 1326(DTJ);
<u>Mississippi</u> - Near Picayune, 4. xii. 1976, Jeannie, Tiffan, and David T. Jenkins and Bill Cibula 1358(DTJ).

Extra-limital:

Guatamala:
Chichicastenango, 20. vii. 1976, Steve Pollock 1330(DTJ).
Mexico:
Desierto del Leon, viii. 1969, Rolf Singer M8900(F).

Nomenclature: At the present the location of the type specimen is not known. In the original article it is listed as being at the University of Michigan Herbarium. A search by Drs. Robert Shaffer and Alexander Smith proved negative. Dr. Singer is currently attempting to locate this specimen. Another specimen collected by Dr. Singer near the type locality was examined. If the type is not located a neotype will be designated.

Observations: This taxon seems to be very common along the southern portion of the United States, but also extending up into the southern Appalachians and the western, coastal states. I have had several reports of it occurring in abundance in south Alabama, Mississippi, Louisiana, and down into Mexico.

At the request of Dr. William G. Cibula I recently visited a U. S. Forest Service loblolly pine plantation near Picayune, Ms. and collected members of this taxon in abundance. During a previous visit to the plantation Dr. Cibula fund an enormous quantity of specimens. In conjunction with remote sensing studies his assistants counted over 9000 specimens in this 20 acre plantation.

At first glance members of this taxon may be mistaken for members of variety *muscaria* because of the red to orange-red pileus. Closer examination reveals the distinctly yellow volval material, as opposed to the white material found on variety *muscaria*. In addition there is a much greater abundance of clamps on the hyphae of variety *flavivolvata* than var. *muscaria*, especially in the subhymenium and on the basidia.

The toxicology of members of this taxon has been examined by Pollock, Jenkins, and Chilton (manuscript in preparation). The presence of muscimol has been confirmed which indicates the presence of ibotenic acid in fresh fruit bodies.

8e. *Amanita muscaria* var. *persicina* Jenkins, var. nov.

Holotype: (Illust. plates 7, 30), Tennessee - Cades Cove, GSMNP, 25. ix. 1973, Priscella Campbell and David T. Jenkins 671(DTJ).

Pileus rufulus in sanguineo ad centrum convertens in flammeolo aut fulvo in margine; volvae suffluvae-fusculae in fusculae; lamellae cum suppuniceo colore; stipes caro suffluva quando secata; volvae pulverulenta; basidia abunde conficta. Typus. Jenkins and Campbell 671 (671); legit prope Cades Cove, Great Smoky Mountains National Park, Tennessee.

Fruit bodies small to medium, slender, solitary. Pileus 4-10 cm diam, hemispherical to truncate-convex when young becoming plano-convex to slightly plano-depressed, faintly to moderately striate, pastel red "M" to light orange "M" or melon "M" on disc to light orange "M" or pale orange to maize yellow "R" on margin, subviscid, glabrous, margin sometimes slightly appendiculate, flesh up to 1 cm thick at center, yellow to pinkish beneath pileipellis, becoming white below; volval remnants as thin, floccose-fibrillose patches at center, becoming more fibrillose toward margin, relatively firmly attached, often in near concentric rings, having a pale yellow tint in buttons but becoming tan in mature fruit bodies. Lamellae very crowded, truncately free, moderately broad, creamy but with a pale, pinkish tint, edges very floccose; lamellulae numerous, abruptly truncate. Stipe 4-10.5 x 0.8-2 cm, cylindrical or slightly expanded at apex, densely stuffed, fibrillose near apex, a pale yellow, but whitish to tannish-white over rest of stipe, becoming fibrous-lacerate near base, flesh turning yellow when cut; basal bulb subglobose to ovoid, 1.5-3.5 x 2-4.5 cm, creamy white to pale buff; volva occasionally as a few very fine ringlets of yellowish-tan to tan, floccose material, or more often, as a thin layer of pulverulent material covering upper portion of bulb and lower stipe; annulus present or absent, near median, either membranous, delicate, whitish above and yellowish below, with a thick edge, often adhering to stipe, or as a very narrow, firm rim, tan, near base. No distinct smell or taste.

Hyphae of pileipellis 2-9 μ diam, interwoven to subradial, strongly gelatinized, hyaline to slightly yellowish in alkaline solution. Lamellar trama bilateral; filamentous hyphae moderately branched, frequently clamped; inflated cells clavate to cylindrical, terminal or in short, terminal chains, cells up to 150 μ long; subhymenium ramose, hyphae clamped; basidia 45-62 x 3-11 μ, 4-sterigmate, clamped. Remnants of volva on pileus as a loose to moderately dense tissue of irregularly disposed, terminal chains of inflated cells and single, terminal cells; cells broadly elliptic to ovoid with few subglobose, up to 45 x 64 μ, and some elliptic, oblong-elliptic, astringo-cylindric, clavate, pyriform, up to 20 x 85 μ, most chains having broad cells terminal; filamentous hyphae 3-7 μ diam, abundant, sparsely to moderately branched, sparsely clamped; gloeoplerous hyphae moderately abundant: volval material at base of stipe very similar but with higher ratio of filamentous hyphae and broadly elliptic and ovoid cells. Stipe trama filamentous hyphae 2-10 μ diam, sparsely branched, usually clamped; inflated cells up to 57 x 380 μ, clavate, terminal, longitudinally oriented. Partial veil composed primarily of moderately branched, occasionally clamped hyphae 3-7 μ diam, with terminal, clavate to cylindric, inflated cells, up to 25 x 160 μ.

Spores (7.0)7.9-8.5 x (9.4)10.2-12.7 μ, ($\underline{E}$ = 1.29-1.61; $\underline{E}^m$ = 1.36), broadly elliptic to elongate, adaxially flattened, thin walled, hyaline, spore print color white, nonamyloid; contents guttulate to subgranular; apiculus sublateral, cylindric.

<u>Habitat</u> <u>and</u> <u>distribution</u>: Terrestrial in coniferous and deciduous forests, Tennessee, Alabama and possibly other southeastern states.

Collections examined:

<u>United States</u>:
<u>Alabama</u> - Childersburg, 12. x. 1975, David T. Jenkins 1107(DTJ); Chase Lake Golf Course, Birmingham, 18. x. 1975, David T. Jenkins 1133b(DTJ); Chase Lake Golf Course, Birmingham, 18. x. 1975, David T. Jenkins 1135(DTJ); Chase Lake Golf Course, Birmingham, 18. x. 1975, David T. Jenkins 1136(DTJ); Lake Nicol, Tuscaloosa Co., 16. xii. 1975, Tim King 1148(DTJ);
<u>North Carolina</u> - Coweeta Hydrologic Station, 22. viii. 1975, David T. Jenkins 952(DTJ);
<u>Tennessee</u> - Cades Cove, GSMNP, 25. ix. 1973, Priscella Campbell and David T. Jenkins 671(DTJ); Cades Cove, 5. x. 1973, David T. Jenkins 718(DTJ); Gatlinburg, 14. x. 1973, David T. Jenkins 720

(DTJ); Gatlinburg, 16. x. 1973, David T. Jenkins 726(DTJ); Cades Cove, 18. x. 1973, David T. Jenkins 727(DTJ).

Observations: *Amanita muscaria* var. *persicina* is a consistently distinct taxon. Several characters, such as spore size, disposition of volval remnants on the pileus, double-edged but collapsible annulus, and the general stature, firmly indicate a relationship with the *A. muscaria* complex. This relationship is solidified by the discovery of muscimol in dried fruit bodies of this variety. Since muscimol is the product of decarboxylation of ibotenic acid, the above implies the presence of ibotenic acid in fresh fruit bodies. I am indebted to Dr. Scott Chilton, University of Washington, for the above determinations.

Of the differences color is the most distinct, being pastel red "M" to melon "M" on the disc, becoming light to pale orange "M" to maize yellow "R" on the margin, even in immature fruit bodies. The volval material has a yellow tint on immature fruit bodies becoming tan with age. This is common for similar structures in var. *alba*. The lamellae have a distinct coloration, being primarily cream but with a definite pale pink tint. Moreover, the volval material at the base usually remains only as a thin pulverulent layer or is completely lacking. Rarely are there faint, irregular ringlets of volval material. A yellowish color is produced in the flesh of the stipe when cut, again a similarity to var. *alba*. Finally, a higher proportion of basidia seem to be clamped than in the other subspecific taxa of *A. muscaria*.

There is a strong possibility that the taxon described here is *A. muscaria* var. *americana* Lange. This taxon appears to be, however, nomenclaturally dubious. To my knowledge this subspecific taxon has never been validly published. The type is an unpublished plate in the possession of Dr. Morten Lange, which I have not seen.

In Lange's first mention of var. *americana* (1934) he only described the pileus color as having an orange-yellow color. With this incomplete description the way was left open for numerous interpretations of the taxon. Gilbert (1941) indicated that *A. roseotinctus* (Murr.), which has amyloid spores, was synonymous with *A. muscaria* var. *americana*. Coker (1917) described specimens under the name *A. muscaria* which, superficially, parallel the description of A. *muscaria* var. *persicina*, but examination of the notes with some of his herbarium specimens reveals the volva as being violaceous. Finally, many herbarium specimens with orange to orange-red pilei, such as A. *muscaria* var. *formosa*, A. *frostiana*, and A. *parcivolvata*, have frequently been misidentified as A. *muscaria* var. *americana*.

Because the taxon proposed is consistently distinct from other varieties, I feel that the introduction of a new name will help stabilize the nomenclature and aid in identification.

9a. *Amanita pantherina* var. *pantherina* (DC. per Fr.) Krombh. 1836. Abbild. 4: pl. 29.

≡ *Agaricus pantherinus* (DC.) Fr. 1821. Syst. Mycol. 1: 16-17.

[≡ *Agaricus pantherinus* DC. 1815. Fl. Francaise 6: 52; deval name].

≡ *Venenarius pantherinus* (DC. per Fr.) Murr. 1913. Mycologia 5: 80.

= *Agaricus maculatus* f. *robusta* Roq. 1774. Hist. Champ.: 318, pl. 20, fig. 3.

= *Amanita pantherina* f. *robusta* Pearson. 1946. Trans. Brit. Mycol. Soc. 29(4): 191-192.

[= *Agaricus maculatus* Schaeff. 1774. Fung. Bav. 4: 39, pl. 90; deval. name].

= *Hypophyllum margaritiferum* Paul. 1778. Soc. Med. t. 12, 14: fig. 2; deval. name .

[= *Agaricus ruderatus* Batsch. 1783. Elen. Fung.: 59; deval. name].

[= *Amanita umbrina* Pers. 1797. Tent. Disp. Meth. Fung.: 67; deval. name].

[≡ *Amanita pustulatus* Schum. 1803. Enum. Pl. Saell.: 251; deval. name].

Type: (Illust, 8, 31), There is no known type specimen for this taxon. A neotype should be selected from material from Switzerland.

Fruit bodies small to large, usually slender, solitary to subgregarious. Pileus 3-16 cm diam, hemispherical to convex, becoming plano-convex to plane, occasionally slightly depressed in center, faintly to strongly striate, blackish-brown, soot brown, dark brown, to olivaceous-brown "R" on disc, becoming pale brown to yellowish-brown near margin, rarely whitish, viscid, glabrous, flesh up to 1.5 cm at center, tapering toward margin of pileus, white with occasional yellow tint just underneath pileipellis; volval remnants as soft, white, floccose patches, irregularly-shaped scales, or pyramidal warts, usually white to pallid, usually randomly arranged, frequently denser at the center, usually becoming more flocculent nearer the margin, which is occasionally slightly appendiculate. Lamellae white to whitish, free to adnexed or attached by a decurrent, floccose line, crowded, broadest near the margin, narrowed at the stipe, edges often floccose or crenulate; lamellulae truncate. Stipe 4-18 x 0.8-2.5 cm, equal or tapering upward, often slightly expanded at apex, white to slightly creamy, stuffed to near hollow, longitudinally fibrous, often with lacerate, reflexed, floccose scales below the annulus and nearer the base, nearly smooth to light floccose above; bulb subglobose to ovoid , 1.5-4 cm thick, white to pallid; volva often as an abrupt margin, flat collar or rolled margin, or occasionally as a thinner, free margin, shallow to 1 cm deep, occasionally with slight ringlets on the lower part of the stipe, white to pallid. Annulus superior to median, membranous, pendant, white or with occasional yellowish-white tint, floccose, edges thickened and torn, persistent, rarely exannulate. No distinct smell or taste.

Hyphae of pileipellis 2-7 μ diam, interwoven to subradial, slightly to strongly gelatinized, hyaline to slightly yellowish in alkaline solution. Lamellar trama bilateral; filamentous hyphae 3-8 μ diam, moderately branched, rarely clamped; inflated cells elongate, terminal and short, terminal chains, up to 160 μ long; subhymenium ramose to slightly inflated-ramose, hyphae rarely clamped; basidia 43-62 x 3-12.6 μ, 4-sterigmate, very rarely clamped. Remnants of volva on pileus a loose to fairly dense tissue of irregularly disposed to apico-basal, terminal chains of inflated cells and single, terminal cells; cells globose, subglobose, broadly elliptic, to ovoid, up to 76 x 95 μ, with oblong-elliptic, clavate, fusiform, cylindric, up to 76 x 159 μ; filamentous hyphae 2-9 μ diam, sparsely to moderately branched, abundant, rarely clamped: volval material at base very similar to that on pileus. Stipe trama filamentous hyphae 2-8 μ diam, sparsely to moderately branched, rarely clamped; inflated cells up to 32 x 320 μ, clavate to elliptic, terminal, longitudinally oriented.

Partial veil filamentous hyphae 2-8 μ diam, moderately branched, rarely clamped, with only occasional short, terminal clavate to cylindric inflated cells.

Spores (6.3)7-9.4(10.2) x (7.9)9.4-12.5(13.9) μ, (E = 1.17-1.62; E^m = 1.32), broadly elliptic to elliptic, adaxially flattened, thin walled, hyaline, spore print color white, nonamyloid; contents guttulate to subgranular; apiculus sublateral, cylindric to truncate-conic.

Habitat and distribution: Terrestrial, frequently under conifers and occasionally under hardwoods, spring and fall, primarily in the western states, occasionally in the eastern states, Canada, and northern and central Europe.

Collections examined:

Canada:
British Columbia - Vancouver, 1. vii. 1959, R. J. Bandoni 494 (UBC);
Ontario - Pembroke, 26. ix. 1968, E. J. Klatt and J. W. Groves 124783(DAOM).

United States:
California - Sierra Co., no date, W. J. Sundberg and Gary Breckon 356(HDT); San Mateo Co., 5. ii. 1965, H. D. Thiers 12170(HDT); Mendocino Co., 18. xi. 1961, H. D. Thiers 882(HDT); Trinidad, 5. vii. 1935, A. H. Smith 3831(MICH); San Jose Pacifica, 21. viii. 76, Steve Pollock 13223(DTJ); San Jose Pacifica, 21. viii. 76, Steve Pollock 1325(DTJ);
Washington - Olympic Mtns., 2. xii. 1941, A. H. Smith 17515(MICH).

Extra-limital:

France -
Pontarlier, 27. viii. 1905, G. F. Atkinson and E. Boudier 20789 (CUP).
Sweden:
Flottsund, 22. viii. 1936, Fungi Exs. Suecici, S. Lundell and J. A. Nannfeldt 304(S); Slottsskogen, 16. ix. 1957, Fungi Exs. Suecici, S. Lundell and J. A. Nannfeldt 2703(S).

Nomenclature: I was able to locate type specimens for any of the taxa cited in the protologue. At the time the older names were proposed, the type concept was not totally accepted.

Observations: *Amanita pantherina* is one of the more easily defined taxa found in section *Amanita*, due to several distinctive characters. One of the more taxonomically important features is the disposition of the volva as an abruptly marginate or rolled collar at the top of the basal bulb, although occasionally the volva shows a thinner, free margin. In some instances ringlets of volval material are found on the lower stipe. The color of the pileus is characteristically dark brown, becoming lighter toward the margin. In addition the pileus margin is usually distinctly striate, with the volval remnants on the pileus being characteristically delicate, floccose patches. These characters, along with an $\underline{E^m}$ range for the spores of 1.27-1.37, readily separates A. *pantherina* from other taxa in this section.

A relationship between A. *pantherina* and A. *muscaria* has frequently been postulated based on toxicological similarities. This relationship has been supported by the studies of Benedict, Tyler, and Brady (1966) and Chilton and Ott (1976).

Amanita pantherina appears to be more or less geographically specific. It is primarily found in the western United States and Canada, with only a few reports indicating the occurrence of this outside the western area (Beardslee, 1934; Atkinson, 1897; Gilbertson, 1966). This corresponds to the apparent limited geographical ranges of other varieties of A. *pantherina*, with var. *pantherinoides* occurring mostly in the western states and var. *velatipes* and *multisquamosa* being found primarily in the eastern and southeastern states.

9b. *Amanita pantherina* var. *multisquamosa* (Pk.) Jenkins stat. nov.
Basionym: *Amanita multisquamosa* Pk. 1900. Ann. Rep. N. Y. St. Mus. 53: 840, pl. B., fig. 1-7.
= *Amanita cothurnata* Atk. 1900. Stud. Amer. Fung.: 66-69 [!] .
 ≡ *Venenarius cothurnatus* (Atk.) Murr. 1913. Mycologia 5: 74.
 ≡ *Amanita pantherina* "f.s." *cothurnata* (Atk.) Gilb. 1941. Icono. Mycol. 27(2): 270.
= *Amanita glabriceps* Pk. 1909. Bull. N. Y. St. Mus. 131: 18,

pl. u [!].

≡ *Venenarius glabricpes* (Pk.) Murr. 1914. North Amer. Fl. 10(1): 72.

Lectotype (Illust. plates 9, 16, 21, 22, 32) (des mihi): New York - Amagansett, Suffolk Co., vii., C. H. Peck s.n. (NYS) [!].

Fruit bodies small to medium, usually slender, solitary to subgregarious. Pileus 3-9 cm diam, hemispherical to convex, becoming plano-convex to occasionally plano-depressed, faintly to strongly striate, usually white with tannish disc, viscid, strongly so when moist, glabrous, flesh usually 1 cm or less at center of pileus, tapering toward margin and becoming very thin; volval remnants as soft, white, angular to diffuse patches, or occasionally angular warts, always becoming more diffuse toward margin, easily removed, numerous and randomly arranged. Lamellae white, free to remote, often rounded next to the stipe, crowded, broadest near nargin, tapering toward stipe, edges often fibrillose or eroded; lamellulae truncate. Stipe 3.5-13 x 0.3-1.2 cm, cylindric or tapering upward, usually slightly expanded at apex, surface minutely to strongly floccose to fibrillose-scaly, white to creamy white, usually hollow; basal bulb usually subglobose to ovoid, rarely over 2.5 cm diam, white to cream; volva frequently forming a distinct collar or roll at apex of bulb, or as a thin, shallow, free margin, never breaking up into rings of material on lower stipe, occasionally forming a narrow neck up to 1 cm up stipe before forming collar or roll, white to whitish. Annulus superior to median, floccose-membranous, often flaring becoming pendant, usually double-edged and ragged, white with edge occasionally yellowish, persistent. Smell and taste not distinctive.

Hyphae of pileipellis 2-9 μ diam, interwoven to subradial, slightly to strongly gelatinized, hyaline to slightly yellowish in alkaline solution. Lamellar trama bilateral; filamentous hyphae up to 9 μ diam, moderately branched, occasionally clamped; inflated cells up to 160 μ long, terminal or short, terminal chains, clavate, fusiform, to oblong-elliptic; hyphae of subhymenium ramose to slightly inflated, hyphae rarely clamped; basidia up to 4-11 x 37-62 μ, 4-sterigmate, rarely clamped. Remnants of volva on pileus a loose to fairly dense tissue of apico-basal to irregularly disposed, terminal chains of inflated cells, or single, terminal cells; cells globose, subglobose, broadly elliptic to ovoid, up to 51 x 60 µ, and elliptic, oblong-elliptic, fusiform, and clavate cells up to 20 x 110 µ, with chains usually terminated by a broadly shaped cell; filamentous hyphae 3-8 µ diam, moderately branched, rarely clamped: volval material at base of stipe very similar to that on the pileus, but with a larger ratio of elongate cells, or with all cells being elongate, up to 25 x 180 µ, but always with filamentous hyphae composing a majority of tissue. Stipe trama filamentous hyphae 2-7 µ diam, sparsely to moderately branched, occasionally clamped; inflated cells up to 40 x 385 µ, clavate to elliptic, terminal, longitudinally oriented. Partial veil mostly filamentous hyphae, 2-7 µ diam, moderately branched, rarely clamped, with terminal, clavate to cylindric, inflated cells, up to 20 x 180 µ.

Spores 6.3-7.9(8.7) x 8.7-11(11.8) µ, ($\underline{E}$ = 1.10-1.49; $\underline{E}^m$ = 1.25), subglobose to elliptic, adaxially flattened, thin walled, hyaline, spore print color white, nonamyloid, contents guttulate to subgranular; apiculus sublateral, cylindric to truncate-conic.

Habitat and distribution: Terrestrial, under conifers and hardwoods, usually occurring during summer and fall, found abundantly in the Southeastern States, also occasionally in the northeastern, midwestern, and northwestern coastal states.

Collections examined:

United States:
Alabama - Auburn, 1. viii. 1955, L. R. Hesler 21952(TENN); Round Forest Dr., Birmingham, 8. ix. 76, David T. Jenkins and Mary Ellen MacDonald 1290(DTJ);
Iowa - Iowa City, 29. ix. 1936, G. W. Martin s.n.(FH);
Maryland - xi., Miss A. Roberna Taylor, (as A. *multisquamosa*), s.n.(NYS);
Michigan - Detroit, 25. vii. 1905, O. E. Fischer 19362(CUP); Pellston, 11. viii. 1951, H. D. Thiers 1269(HDT); Pellston, 18. vii. 1955, H. D. Thiers 2552(HDT);
New York - Amagansett, Suffolk Co., vii., C. H. Peck, (as A. *multisquamosa*), s.n.(NYS); Bolton Landing, viii., C. H. Peck, (as A. *multisquamosa*), s.n.(NYS); Round Lake, viii. C. H. Peck, (as A. *multisquamosa*), s.n.(NYS); Greenbush, viii., C. H. Peck, (as A.

multisquamosa), s.n.(NYS); Rensslaer Co., no date, E. A. Perine, (as A. *glabriceps*), s.n.(NYS); Steuben Co., 7. viii. 1908, C. H. Peck, (as A. *glabriceps*), s.n.(NYS);

<u>North Carolina</u> - Blowing Rock, ix. 1899, G. F. Atkinson 3715(CUP-A); Blowing Rock, 19. viii. - 22. ix. 1901, C. Meedom 10303(CUP); Franklin, 16. viii. 1936, L. R. Hesler and A. J. Sharp 9228(TENN); Highlands, 15. vii. 1955, L. R. Hesler 21898(TENN); Yellow Gap Rd., 12. viii. 1971, David T. Jenkins 383(DTJ); Pink Beds, 12. viii. 1971, David T. Jenkins 384(DTJ); Macon Co., viii. 1964, R. H. Petersen 27536(TENN); Macon Co., 22. viii. 1975, David, Jeannie, and Tiffan Jenkins 999(DTJ);

<u>Pennsylvania</u> - Bethlehem, ix., C. H. Peck s.n.(NYS);

<u>Tennessee</u> - Norris, 26. vi. 1965, L. R. Hesler 28063(TENN); Cades Cove, GSMNP, 15. viii. 1972, David T. Jenkins 681(DTJ); Unaka Mtns., 7. viii. 1973, David T. Jenkins 670(DTJ); Cades Cove, GSMNP, 14. viii. 1948, L. R. Hesler 18566(TENN); Cades Cove, GSMNP, 9. vii. 1963, L. R. Hesler 25623 (TENN); Cosby, 30. vii. 1936, L. R. Hesler and A. J. Sharp 9004(TENN); Norris, 4. vii. 1960, L. R. Hesler 23720(TENN); Cades Cove, GSMNP, 1. vii. 1971, David T. Jenkins 234(DTJ); Roaring Fork, GSMNP, 9. vii. 1971, David T. Jenkins 270(DTJ); Montvale springs, 18. vi. 1935, L. R. Hesler 7779(TENN); Ball Camp Pike, 21. vii. 1936, L. R. Hesler and A. J. Sharp 8988(TENN); Elkmont, GSMNP, 13. vi. 1937, L. R. Hesler 10-405(TENN); Elkmont, GSMNP, 28. vii. 1971, L. R. Hesler 24600 (TENN).

<u>Nomenclature</u>: My studies indicate that A. *multisquamosa* and A. *cothurnata* are synonymous. The only significant difference between the two original descriptions was the lack of the cothurnate, volval roll in A. *multisquamosa*. But I have examined specimens intermediate between the volval roll of A. *cothurnata* and the thinner, volval margin of A. *multisquamosa*. Therefore, no characters of taxonomic importance were sufficiently different to allow for two separate taxa.

This synonymy, however, means that the epithet *multisquamosa* is the valid name (Lanjouw, 1966; Art. 11, 60A), even though the epithet *cothurnata* is much more commonly used.

The same principle holds true for A. *glabriceps* because of its later date of publication.

Observations: It has been widely published that A. *cothurnata* Atk. is related to A. *pantherina* (Beardslee, 1914; Gilbert, 1941a; Smith, 1958). Beardslee said that A. *cothurnata* was the American expression of the European A. *pantherina*. At the time he had not seen A. *pantherina* in North America. Gilbert also felt that A. *cothurnata* was the American version of A. *pantherina*. He stated, "La constance des characteres, l'abondance relative et la large distribution de cette *Amanite* dans l'Amerique du Nord obligent a la maintenir dans la classification." Therefore, it was designated as a "forma specialis" (Lanjouw, 1966; Art. 4) producing A. *pantherina* f.s. *cothurnata*.

I perceive a consistency of characters that warrants nomenclatural status greater than the "forma specialis" of Gilbert. The pileus color in the taxon is consistently white to pale cream with an occasional pale tannish disc, as compared to A. *pantherina's* consistently darker brown pileus. Also there seems to be a fairly distinct geographical separation of these two taxa, with A. *cothurnata* (= A. *pantherina* var. *multisquamosa*) occurring primarily in the eastern and southeastern states and A. *pantherina* occurring primarily in the western states. In addition the spores of var. *multisquamosa* are slightly smaller.

9c. *Amanita pantherina* var. *pantherinoides* (Murr.) Jenkins stat. nov.
Basionym: *Venenarius pantherinoides* Murr. 1912. Mycologia 4: 242.
≡ *Amanita pantherinoides* (Murr.) Sacc. 1925. Syll. Fung. 23: 2.
(cf. *Amanita pantherinoides* Murr. 1912. Mycologia 13: 271; *Amanita pantherinoides* Murr. 1912. Mycologia 4: 262).
= *Amanita praegemmata* (Murr.) Sacc. 1925. Syll. Fung. 23: 3 [!].
≡ *Venenarius praegemmatus* Murr. 1912. Mycologia 4: 243.
(cf. *Amanita praegemmata* Murr. 1912. Mycologia 4: 262).
Holotype: Washington - near Seattle, 20. x. - 1. xi. 1911, W. A. Murrill 399(NY) [!].

Fruit bodies small to medium, slender solitary. Pileus 3-10 cm diam, globose to hemispherical, becoming plane, faintly striate to non-striate, melleous to dirty-cremeous with brown to chestnut "R" to melleous-avellaneous "R" disc, viscid when wet, glabrous, flesh relatively thin, tapering toward margin of pileus; volval remnants as soft, small, white, floccose-fibrillose patches and warts, numerous and randomly distributed until falling away, becoming diffuse toward margin. Lamellae white, narrowly adnexed to free, connected to stipe by an extremely heavy, floccose line, crowded, broadest near margin, narrowed toward stipe; lamellulae truncate. Stipe 2-11 x 0.5-1.1 cm, tapering upward, often slightly expanded at apex, white to whitish, stuffed to nearly hollow, glabrous; basal bulb ovoid, white, smooth to minutely floccose; volva usually with appressed to adnate, white to whitish, floccose material often around base of stipe and/or with entire or undulate, free margin, usually slight, often with floccose material at apex of bulb. Annulus relatively large, white, superior but not apical, persistent, sometimes adhering slightly to margin of pileus.

Hyphae of pileipellis 2-8 µ diam, interwoven to subradial, slightly to strongly gelatinized, hyaline to slightly yellowish in alkaline solution. Lamellar trama bilateral; filamentous hyphae 3-8 µ diam, moderately branched, rarely clamped; inflated cells clavate to irregularly elongate, terminal or short, terminal chains, up to 110 µ long; subhymenium ramose to inflated ramose, hyphae rarely clamped; basidia up to 4.5-12.5 x 40-50 µ, 4-sterigmate, rarely clamped. Remnants of volva on pileus a fairly loose tissue of apico-basal to irregularly disposed, terminal chains of inflated cells and single, terminal cells; cells subglobose, broadly elliptic, to ovoid, up to 57 x 83 µ, and elliptic, clavate, to irregularly elongate, up to 55 x 115 µ; filamentous hyphae up to 7 µ diam, moderately branched, moderately abundant, rarely clamped: volval material at base of stipe very similar to that on the pileus but with a greater ratio of elongate cells, these mostly cylindric, clavate, or oblong-elliptic. Stipe trama filamentous hyphae up to 6 µ diam, sparsely branched, rarely clamped; inflated cells up to 32 x 286 µ, clavate to fusiform-elliptic, terminal, longitudinally oriented. Partial veil almost completely filamentous hyphae; hyphae up to 6 µ diam, moderately branched, rarely clamped; inflated cells up to 25 x 130 µ, terminal, clavate to cylindric.

Spores 6.3-7.9 x 8.7-10.2(11) µ, ($\underline{E}$ = 1.34-1.62; $\underline{E}^m$ = 1.51), elliptic to elongate, adaxially flattened, thin walled, hyaline, spore print color white, nonamyloid, contents guttulate to subgranular; apiculus sublateral, cylindric to truncate-conic.

Habitat and distribution: Terrestrial, under conifers and hardwoods, late summer and fall, wet coastal forests of northwestern states.

Collections examined:

United States:
Washington - Seattle, 20. x.-1. xi. 1911, W. A. Murrill 399(NY); Seattle, 20. x.-1. xi. 1911, W. A. Murrill, (as A. praegemmata), 247(NY); Seattle, 20. x.-1. xi. 1911, W. A. Murrill, (as A. praegemmata), 548(NY); Seattle, 20. x.-1. xi. 1911, W. A. Murrill, (as A. praegemmata), 646(NY).

Nomenclature: Although A. pantherinoides and A. praegemmata were proposed by Murrill in the same publication I chose the epithet pantherinoides for this variety because it implied a greater affinity to the A. pantherina group than did the epithet praegemmata.

The credit for the combinations Amanita pantherinoides and Amanita praegemmata is given to Saccardo (1925) and not Murrill. In his publications Murrill (1912a; 1912b) frequently listed at the end of each artical the epithet he had given to the taxon described in combination under Amanita, "for those who follow Saccardo." He obviously did not intend for these combinations to be accepted (Lanjouw, 1966; Art. 33, 34).

The use of Amanita pantherinoides by Krieger (1921) is only an incidental mention of the taxon and cannot be considered a valid publication of a new combination.

Observations: It is obvious that var. pantherinoides has a very close affinity with the A. pantherina complex, including color and stature. There are several consistent differences, however, that I feel warrant recognition as a separate taxon. There is a consistent difference in the $\underline{E}^m$ values of the spores. I have found the $\underline{E}^m$ value for var. pantherina to be 1.32, while that of var. pantherinoides is 1.51. Also var. pantherinoides does not have as distinctly the abruptly margined or rolled volva collar at the top of the basal bulb as found in var. pantherina.

Instead it appears to be more closely appressed with a thinner, free margin. In addition the pileus is faintly or not striate. When considering the similarities between the two varieties the above character differences alone are not sufficient to delimit an autonomous species, but in my estimation justify recognition at the varietal level.

Gilbert (1941a) stated that *Amanita pantherinoides* and *A. pantherina* f.s. *abietum* Gilb. apud Konr. & Maubl are synonyms. Not having examined a sufficient number of f.s. *abietum* specimens to become familar with the taxon I must reserve judgement on this possible synonymy. The same principle applies to Gilbert's suggestion (1941a) that *A. praegemmata* is synonymous with *A. gemmata* f. *amici* (Gillet) Gilbert.

6d. *Amanita pantherina* var. *velatipes* (Atk.) Jenkins. stat. nov. Basionym: *Amanita velatipes* Atk. 1900. Stud. Amer. Fung.: 63-66, figs. 64-67.

≡ *Venenarius velatipes* (Atk.) Murr. 1913. Mycologia 5: 75.

Neotype (Illust. plates 10, 33) (des. mihi): New York - Cayuga Lake Basin, 28. vii. 1897, Hasselbring 3167(CUP) [!].

Fruit bodies medium to large, slender, solitary to subgregarious. Pileus 7-15 cm diam, hemispherical to oval to convex then plane, with margin occasionally elevated with age, moderately to strongly striate, usually rich hair brown "R" to umber brown, being darker on disc, occasionally light brown or becoming a dull maize yellow "R" on disc, fading to a paler yellow or cream toward the margin, viscid when moist, glabrous, flesh rather thin, tapering toward and becoming very thin on pileus margin; volval remnants white or cream, never yellow, always lighter than pileus, flattened, thin, angular, floccose patches, more often warts on disc, at first transversely elongate, becoming isodiametric as pileus expands, the margin of the remnants reflexed with age and easily removed, often randomly arranged in near concentric rings. Lamellae white, close, free, connected to stipe by a faint, floccose line, broad near the middle, tappering toward both ends; lamellulae truncate. Stipe 8-20 x 0.8-2 cm, cylindric or tapering slightly upwards, white, hollow or stuffed with loose, cottonly threads, smooth or slightly fibrillose above, becoming strongly fibrous or lacerate with recurved, fibrous scales near base; basal bulb ovoid to subradicate, up to 2.5 x 4 cm, white to pallid; volva usually ocreate or cothurnate, often having sturdy limbs up to 1 cm deep, these limbs being floccose-membranous with other floccose patches around apex of bulb and occasionally on lower part of stipe, white to cream. Annulus median to inferior, rarely superior, at first flaring, then pendant after collapsing from attachment to pileus margin, white, margin irregular, occasionally thickened, persistent, often torn longitudinally for entire length of annulus.

Hyphae of pileipellis 2-8 µ diam, interwoven to subradial, slightly to strongly gelatinized. Pileus trama composed of undifferentiated hyphae; inflated cells clavate to irregularly elongate, terminal and short, terminal chains, cells up to 32 x 222 µ. Lamellar trama bilateral; hyphae 2-7 µ diam, moderately branched, rarely clamped; inflated cells up to 51 x 191 µ, clavate, fusiform, to irregularly elongate, terminal and short, terminal chains; subhymenial hyphae ramose, occasionally clamped; basidia 39-50 x 4-11 µ, 4-sterigmate, rarely clamped. Remnants of volva on pileus a loose to fairly dense tissue of irregularly disposed to occasional apico-basal, terminal chains of inflated cells and single, terminal cells; cells globose, subglobose, ovoid, to broadly elliptic, up to 57 x 64 µ, with oblong-elliptic, elliptic, clavate, fusiform, up to 38 x 95 µ; filamentous hyphae 2-9 µ diam, abundant, moderately branched, occasionally clamped: volva at the stipe base somewhat similar to that on pileus, often with fewer inflated cells. Stipe trama hyphae 3-6 µ diam, sparsely to moderately branched, rarely clamped; inflated cells up to 38 x 450 µ, with a tendency to be long and slender, clavate, terminal, longitudinally oriented. Partial veil composed of terminal, clavate to elliptic inflated cells; cells up to 45 x 191 µ, with only occasional broader cells; filamentous hyphae 2-8 µ diam, sparsely to moderately branched, rarely clamped, with a majority of the velar tissue usually being composed of slender hyphae.

Spores 6.3-7.9 x (7.9)8.7-11(13.2) µ, (E = 1.25-1.71; E^m = 1.43), broadly elliptic to elongate, often adaxially flattened, smooth, thin walled, hyaline, spore print color white, nonamyloid; contents guttulate; apiculus sublateral, cylindric to truncate-conic.

<u>Habitat and distribution:</u> Terrestrial, in mixed woods,

summer to fall, primarily eastern and southeastern, possibly midwestern states, and southeastern Canada.

Collections examined:

Canada:
Ontario - Lake Poinicon, 27. ix. 1958, J. W. Groves 59988(DAOM); Goose Bay, Labrador, 4. viii. 1950, S. C. Thomson 25026(DAOM).

United States:
Connecticut - Farmington, 1900, Miss Mary Smith 8359(CUP);
Maryland - Baltimore, vii. or viii. 1924, H. A. Kelley s.n., H. A. Kelley Herbarium(MICH);
New York - Six Mile Creek, 29. ix. 1912, M. Ishikawa 23462(CUP); Skanaeteles, viii. 1900, G. F. Atkinson 5649(CUP); Six Mile Creek, 18. ix. 1911, Higgins and G. F. Atkinson 23225(CUP); Cayuga Lake Basin, ix. 1900, 15084(CUP); Cayuga Lake Basin, 28. vii. 1897, Hasselbring and G. F. Atkinson 3167(CUP);
Tennessee - Cherokee Orchard, 21. vii. 1940, L. R. Hesler, (as A. *junquillea*), 12711(TENN); Cades Cove, GSMNP, 5. viii. 1954, L. R. Hesler, (as A. *junquillea*), 21464(TENN); Cades Cove, GSMNP, 8. vi. 1957, L. R. Hesler, (as A. *junquillea*), 22582(TENN); Deep Creek, 19. vii. 1961, Ray Hatcher and L. R. Hesler, (as A. *junquillea*), 24407(TENN); Deep Creek, 29. vi. 1962, L. R. Hesler, (as A. *junquillea*), 25650(TENN); Mt. LeConte, GSMNP, 5. viii. 1964, (as A. *junquillea*), 26285(TENN); Wayah Bald, 21. viii. 1955, L. R. Hesler, (as A. *junquillea*), 22038(TENN); Roaring Fork, GSMNP, 12. viii. 1971, David T. Jenkins, (as A. *junquillea*), 272(DTJ); Roaring Folk, GSMNP, 22. viii. 1971, David T. Jenkins, (as A. *junquillea*), 307(DTJ).

Observations: When Atkinson proposed the name A. *velatipes* he used the formation of the annulus as its most distinctive character. He stated that the annulus was formed by "ripping up the outer layers of the stem as the latter elongates and as the pileus expands." Upon examination of specimens of this taxon, however, there was no evidence to support this peculiar formation. The elongate cells frequently found in the annuli of specimens are not exceptionally long as might be excepted if they were torn from the stipe.

Examination of several characters, especially the volva structures and its disposition on the base of the stipe, clearly shows a relationship with A. *pantherina*. The volva is always abruptly margined or with a thick, free margin with occasional ringlets of volva tissue on the lower stipe. The lower portion of the stipe is also occasionally lacerate with reflexed scales. In addition the decarboxylated form of the toxin ibotenic acid, muscimol, has been detected in specimens of var. *velatipes* (Pollock, Jenkins, and Chilton; manuscript in preparation).

There are several features, however, that differ sufficiently to warrant a separate taxon. The color of the pileus varies from an umber brown to a tannish-yellow on the disc with a pale yellowish-brown to a cream on the margin. The volva remnants on the pileus are denser than the more delicate floccose patches of A. *pantherina*. The scales often become upturned on the margin and are easily removed. The spores are more elongate, with an $\underline{E^m}$ value occasionally exceeding 1.5. Finally, as in A. *pantherina* var. *multisquamosa*, this taxon seems to be primarily limited to the eastern and southeastern United States and eastern Canada.

Included within this taxon are large specimens frequently found in the southeast and popularly identified as A. *junquillea*.

This taxon appears to be very similar to A. *gemmata* f. *amici* (Gilb., 1941b). Since I was unable to examine any authentic material of f. *amici*, however, I hesitate at this time to accept the synonymy.

10. *Amanita parcivolvata* (Pk.) Gilbert. 1941. Bresadola Icono. Mycol. 27(2): 226.

≡ *Amanitopsis parcivolvata* Pk. 1900. Bull. Torr. Bot. Club 27(12): 610.

≡ *Vaginata parcivolvata* (Pk.) Murr. 1913. Mycologia 5: 83.
= *Amanita muscaria* var. *coccinea* Beardslee. 1902. Jour. Elisha Mitch. Soc. 12: 8.

Lectotype (Illust. plates 11, 34) (des. mihi): North Carolina - Skyland, Henderson Co., vii., Miss Mary Wilson s.n.(NYS) [!].

Fruit bodies small to medium, slender, solitary to subgregarious. Pileus 3-12 cm diam, hemispherical to convex, becoming plane to occasionally plano-depressed, margin usually strongly striate to tuberculate-striate, often slightly appendiculate, orange to yellowish-orange, more often crimson on disc, becoming orange, golden yellow "M" to paler yellow on margin, viscid when moist, glabrous, flesh white or white tinged with orange or yellow, reddish-yellow under pileipellis, thin, tapering toward margin; volval remnants as irregularly distributed, floccose-fibrillose warts and patches, more numerous on disc, usually a dirty yellow to rarely cream or white. Lamellae pale yellow "M", free, usually distinctly so with pulverulent material filling the space between the gills and stipe, edges strongly floccose, crowded, broader near the margin, tapering toward the stipe; lamellulae truncate. Stipe 3-12 x 0.3-1.7 cm, tapering slightly upward, expanded at apex, pale yellow "M" to occasionally white, stuffed or hollow, furfuraceous or mealy near apex, becoming more fibrillose toward the base; basal bulb subglobose to subradicate; volva often remaining as loose, floccose material or randomly distributed, floccose patches, rarely having a free margin of floccose-membranous material, more often with no remnants remaining, usually pale yellow "M", rarely white. No annulus present.

Hyphae of pileipellis 2-7 µ diam, interwoven to subradial, slightly gelatinized. Lamellar trama bilateral; filamentous hyphae 3-6 µ diam, moderately branched, clamped, inflated cells up to 31 x 130 µ, elliptic to clavate, terminal or short, terminal chains; subhymenium ramose, hyphae clamped; basidia 40-62 x 4-12.6 µ, 4-sterigmate, rarely clamped. Remnants of volva on pileus a loose to fairly dense tissue of apico-basal to irregularly disposed, terminal chains of inflated cells and single, terminal cells; cells globose, subglobose, ovoid, broadly elliptic, up to 95 x 100 µ, with elliptic, oblong-elliptic, clavate, fusiform, and cylindric, up to 32 x 95 µ; filamentous hyphae 2-10 µ diam, not abundant, sparsely to moderately branched, clamps not common: volval material at stipe base very similar to that on pileus. Stipe trama filamentous hyphae 3-8 µ diam, sparsely to moderately branched, rarely clamped; inflated cells up to 64 x 380 µ, clavate to elliptic, terminal, longitudinally oriented. Floccose-scaly material at apex of stipe composed of randomly distributed, terminal chains of cells; cells globose, subglobose, ovoid, broadly elliptic up to 20 x 32 µ, with elliptic, oblong-elliptic, and clavate, up to 80 x 130 µ; hyphae sparse.

Spores 6.3-7.9 x (9.4)11-12.6(14.1) µ, ($\underline{E}$ = 1.34-2.0; $\underline{E}^m$ =

1.58), elliptic to near cylindric, adaxially flattened, thin walled, hyaline, spore print color white, nonamyloid; contents guttulate; apiculus sublateral, cylindric to occasionally truncate-conic.

Habitat and distribution: Terrestrial, in mixed woods, summer to early fall, primarily the mid-Atlantic to Southeastern states.

Collections examined:

United States:
Alabama - Cherokee Bend, Birmingham, 31. vii. 76, David T. Jenkins 1153(DTJ); Shades Mountain, 16. vii. 76, David T. Jenkins 1195 (DTJ); Mountain Brook, 8. ix. 76, David T. Jenkins 1281(DTJ);
Maryland - Hyattsville, 12. viii. 1960, C. R. Banjamin s.n.(BPI);
North Carolina - Skyland, no date, Miss Mary L. Wilson s.n.(NYS); Chapel Hill, 23. ix. 1945, 13934(NCU): Highlands, 28. vii. 1919, 8932(NCU);
Tennessee - Mountain Crest, Knoxville, no date, David T. Jenkins 567(DTJ); Cades Cove, GSMNP, 5. vii. 1973, David T. Jenkins 622 (DTJ); Fall Creek Falls, 29. vii. 1973, David T. Jenkins 655(DTJ); Crossville, 19. vii. 1972, David T. Jenkins 541(DTJ); Walland, 3. viii. 1964, L. R. Hesler 26274(TENN); Cades Cove, GSMNP, 18, vii. 1958, L. R. Hesler 23050(TENN); Knox Co., 31. vii. 1963, L. R. Hesler 26108(TENN); Oconee Co., 24. vii. 1965, L. R. Hesler 28095 (TENN);
Virginia - Radnor Heights, 28. ix. 1935, C. L. Shear s.n.(BPI).

Nomenclature: The publication of *Amanita muscaria coccinea* by Beardslee (1908) cannot be considered as a valid combination because it is a trinomial (Lanjouw, 1966; Art. 23).
See type studies for lectotypification.

Observations: This is another unusually distinct taxon within section *Amanita*. With its bright red to red-orange pileus color, pale yellow "M" lamellae, and exannulate, yellow pulverulent stipe, it is very difficult to misidentify in the field. The very characteristic yellow pulverulence on the stipe is undoubtedly the result of a poorly developed and incoherent partial veil (Atkinson, 1914).

Beardslee (1902) called this organism *Amanita muscaria* var. *coccinea*. The characters he used to place it in this taxon were the lack of an annulus and the pulverulence on the margin of the gills. Neither of these features is of primary importance in the delineation of *Amanita muscaria* and its subspecific taxa. Undoubtedly the brightly colored pileus and floccose material usually found on the base were also influential in his decision. Several characters clearly separate A. *parcivolvata* from the A. *muscaria* complex, i.e., the yellow lamellae, pulverulent or furfuraceous stipe, and the elongate to near cylindric spores.

11. *Amanita wellsii* (Murr.) Sacc. 1925. Syll. Fung. 13: 2-3.
    ≡ *Venenarius wellsii* Murr. 1920. Mycologia 12: 291-292.
    (cf. *Amanita wellsii* Murr. 1920. Mycologia 12: 292).

Holotype: (Illust. plates 12, 35), New Hampshire - Springfield, "about" 1. ix. 1917, W. A. Murrill s.n.(NY) [!].

Fruit bodies small to medium, usually slender, solitary to subgregarious. Pileus 3-13 cm diam, globose to convex, at length plano-convex to plane, margin not striate at first, but becoming distinctly so in age, often extending beyond the gills about 2-3 mm forming a conspicuous sterile edge, zinc-orange "R" to ochraceous-salmon "R", fading to near antimony yellow "R", remaining darker on disc, surface dry to viscid when moist, flesh yellow beneath pileipellis becoming white below, tapering toward pileus margin; volval remnants as irregularly distributed, delicate warts to soft squamules or patches of easily removable floccose material, often forming a tomentum on the margin, yellowish-buff "R" to cadmium yellow "R", rarely whitish. Lamellae white at first, becoming pale cream to Naples yellow "R", free or adnexed, with occasional, faint, decurrent floccose line, crowded, widest nearer the margin, narrowed toward the stipe, edged distinctly yellowish floccose; lamellulae truncate. Stipe 7-16 x 0.5-2 cm, tapering upward, expanded at apex, pale yellow "M", near baryta yellow "R", stuffed or hollow, furfuraceous above annulus, nearly glabrous below; basal bulb subglobose to ovoid, 1.5-2.5 cm thick, pallid; volva delicate and fragmentary, often as loosely woven, evanescent, floccose patches, or occasionally as a shallow, delicate, free margin, distinctly yellow. Annulus superior, very delicate and loosely woven, evanescent, distinctly yellow, usually adhering to margin of the pileus, leaving only a slight, evanescent ring on stipe, soon disappearing. Taste mild but with a lingering unpleasantness.

Spores 6.3-8.3 x 11-13.3(14.1) μ, (E = 1.39-2.0; E^m = 1.64), elliptic to near cylindric, adaxially flattened, thin walled, hyaline, spore print color white, nonamyloid, contents guttulate; apiculus sublateral, cylindrical.

Habitat and distribution: Terrestrial, in mixed woods, often on road-cuts or other exposed areas, late summer and early fall, New England states, extending down Appalachian Mtn. chain.

Collections examined:

United States:
Maine - Franklin Co., 18. viii. 1971, H. E. Bigelow 37285(TENN);
New Hampshire - Springfield, no date, H. W. Wells s.n.(NY);
North Carolina - NewFound Gap, GSMNP, 10. viii. 1952, L. R. Hesler 21487(TENN); Smokemont, GSMNP, 25. viii. 1952, L. R. Hesler 20522(TENN).

Observations: *Amanita wellsii* seems to be related, at least distantly, to *A. parcivolvata*. This possible relationship is based primarily on the yellowish, floccose volva which is evanescent at the base of the stipe and the elongate to near cylindric spores. The scarcity of filamentous hyphae in the volva produces the delicate nature. Both taxa also tend to have yellowish lamellae. The annulus in *A. wellsii* is slightly more developed than in *A. parcivolvata*, but is still evanescent resulting in an exannulate fruit body in most mature specimens.

Gilbert (1941a) stated that *Venenarius wellsii* Murr. was probably described from small specimens of *Amanita flavorubens* Berk. & Montagen in Montagne. After examining the spores of the holotype of *A. wellsii*, it is evident that these two taxa are not synonymous, since *A. wellsii* has nonamyloid spores and *A. flavorubens* has amyloid spores.

Nomina Dubia:

Amanita pubescens Schw. 1822. Schr. Nat. Ges. Leipzig 1: 79.

I feel that *Amanita pubescens* must be declared a nomen dubium. There does not appear to be a type specimen in existence, and I could not locate any material that was collected by Schweinitz. There is, of course, the possibility that W. C. Coker, who collected in many of the same areas as Schweinitz, had the best concept of A. *pubescens*. Since Coker was not a contemporary of L. D. von Schweinitz, however, I feel that acceptance of Coker's concept would be too arbitrary.

TYPE STUDIES

Type specimens reported here are for taxa named by C. H. Peck, M. J. Berkeley, G. F. Atkinson, W. A. Murrill, and Linnaeus.

The rules of nomenclature followed by today's botanists were either not in existence or not readily complied with during the professional life of most of the early workers. Nomenclatural problems, therefore, accompany many of their names. Most problems originate from methods of specimen citation. Often the information in citations was very vague or there was none, necessitating the later designation of lectotypes or neotypes. The specimens were rarely labeled to indicate a special status, making necessary the selection of one of several candidates. Peck, for example, never designated type specimens. Usually in the original description he cited one or more collecting locales and/or dates, but such citations were almost always very incomplete. When such citations are found, it is usually necessary to designate a neotype because the citation is not complete enough to allow the luxury of a lectotype. Likewise, caution must be exercised in selection of lectotype specimens for names by Atkinson, who often selected type specimens from the herbaria of other investigators.

In the following descriptions the reader is cautioned that the descriptions and measurements were made from material that was quite old and often poorly preserved. Frequently the material being microscopically examined reinflated very poorly, making exact measurements impossible. If the material could not be reinflated to the point of recognition this character is omitted.

1. *Agaricus agglutinatus* Berk. & Curt. in Berk. 1849. Hook Jour. Bot. 1: 97-98.

≡ *Amanita agglutinata* (Berk. & Curt. in Berk.) Llyod. 1898. Volvae p. 9.

Holotype: South Carolina, viii. 1847, M. A. Curtis 1322(K).

Pileus approximately 2 cm diam, flattened, margin striate; volval remnants as many, small warts, mostly flattened. Lamellae free, crowded; lamellulae truncate. Stipe approximately 0.3-0.4 x 1.7 cm, tapering very slightly upward, basal bulb globose, volva irregularly lobed, approximately 2 mm deep, appressed against stipe.

Pileipellis a layer of densely interwoven to subradial, gelatinized hyphae, with gloeoplerous hyphae common. Pileus trama composed of undifferentiated hyphae and inflated cells. Lamellar trama bilateral. Hyphae of volva on pileus approximately 4.6 μ diam, moderately to densely branched, clamp connections not observed; gloeoplerous hyphae abundant; inflated cells broadly elliptic, ovoid, up to 45 x 57 μ, with oblong-elliptic, elliptic, to irregularly elongate up to 15 x 95 μ, usually as randomly oriented, terminal chains: hyphae of volva at base of stipe approximately 3-7 μ diam, moderately branched, no clamps observed, gloeoplerous hyphae abundant; inflated cells up to 35 x 75 μ, primarily clavate to elliptic, and less frequently broadly elliptic, up to 55 x 70 μ, usually in short, randomly oriented chains. Stipe trama hyphae 2-6.5 diam, abundant, sparsely branched; inflated cells oblong-elliptic to clavate, terminal, longitudinally oriented, up to 55 x 145 μ.

Spores 5.5-8 x 9-12.5 μ, (E = 1.40-1.90; $\underline{E}^m$ = 1.62), elliptic to elongate, adaxially flattened, smooth, thin walled, hyaline, nonamyloid; contents guttulate to subgranular; apiculus sublateral, cylindric to truncate-conic, up to 2.5 μ in length.

2. *Amanitopsis albocreata* Atk. 1902. Jour. Mycol. 8: 111-112.

≡ *Amanita albocreata* (Atk.) Gilb. 1941. Iconogr. Mycol. 27(2); 259.

Lectotype (des mihi): New York - Beebe Lake Woods, 12. vii. 1902, H. H. Whetzel 9822(CUP).

Pileus approximately 3-6 cm diam, convex to plano-convex, margin strongly striate; volva as randomly distributed, floccose patches and warts. Lamellae free, crowded; lamellulae truncate.

Stipe 3-6 x 0.2-0.6 cm, tapering upward, stuffed, with ovoid bulb; volva as a very shallow, free margin at apex of bulb or very slight floccose patches at apex.

Pileipellis of interwoven, gelatinized hyphae. Hyphae of pileus trama 3-8 µ diam, moderately branched, rarely clamped; inflated cells clavate or irregularly elongate, up to 20 x 160 µ. Lamellar trama bilateral; hyphae 3-5 µ diam, moderately branched, rarely clamped; inflated cells clavate or irregularly elongate, up to 20 x 150 µ; subhymenial hyphae ramose, rarely clamped; basidia 39-45 x 1.5-11 µ, 4-sterigmate, clamps rare. Hyphae of volva on pileus 3-8 µ diam, moderately branched, rarely clamped; inflated cells subglobose, broadly elliptic, ovoid, pyriform, eleliptic, oblong-elliptic, clavate, up to 38 x 70 µ, arranged as irregularly disposed to apico-basal, terminal chains: hyphae of volva at base 2.5-5 µ diam, moderately branched, rarely clamped; inflated cells broadly elliptic, ovoid, oblong-elliptic, astringo-cylindric, up to 32 x 67 µ, often arranged in terminal chains. Stipe trama hyphae undifferentiated and inconspicuous with terminal, broadly clavate, longitudinally oriented cells, up to 38 x 220 µ.

Spores 6.3-7.9 x 7.0-7.9 µ, ($\underline{E}$ = 1.0-1.25; $\underline{E}^m$ = 1.08), globose to broadly elliptic, smooth, hyaline, thin walled, non-amyloid; contents guttulate; apiculus sublateral, cylindric to truncate-conic.

Typification: In the original description Atkinson cited three specimens, but designated none as type. Therefore, a lectotype must be selected. In agreement with Bas (annotated specimens) the above stated was chosen because it best exemplified the characters originally described, although "part of type" is written on packet no. 9757.

3. *Amanita chrysoblema* Atk. in Kauffman. 1918. Agaricaceae of Michigan: 613-614.

Holotype: Michigan - Chelsea, "On ground in edge of sphagnum swamp," 20. ix. 1907, C. H. Kauffman s.n.(CUP).

Pileus approximately 7 cm diam, plane with margin slightly inrol' 1, margin striate; volva as very thin floccose-flaky layer, quite dense on the disc. Lamellae remote, crowded; lamellulae truncate. Stipe approximately 0.5-0.9 x 11 cm, tapering upward, stuffed, bulbous at base; volva as thin, floccose tissue at apex of base, extending up stipe slightly as floccose patches or rings of patches.

Pileipellis of densely interwoven to subradial, gelatinized hyphae. Hyphae of pileus trama up to 10 μ diam, moderately branched, clamped; inflated cells up to 32 x 160 μ, clavate to irregularly elongate. Lamellar trama bilateral; hyphae undifferentiated; cells inflated; subhymenial hyphae ramose, clamps occasionally present; basidia 40-54 x 4.5-11 μ, clamps occasionally present. Hyphae of volva on pileus very sparse, 3-8 μ diam, moderately branched, clamped; inflated cells up to 25 x 76 μ, globose, subglobse, broadly elliptic, ovoid, elliptic, clavate, and fusiform, arranged in short, randomly oriented, terminal chains; hyphae of volva at base of stipe 3-8 μ diam, moderately branched, abundantly clamped; inflated cells up to 32 x 83 μ, similar in shape to above, arranged in terminal chains. Stipe trama hyphae 2-8 μ diam, moderately branched, occasionally clamped; inflated cells up to 38 x 380 μ, narrowly clavate, terminal, longitudinally oriented.

Spores 6.3-7.0 x 7.9-9.4 μ, ($\underline{E}$ = 1.25-1.49; $\underline{E}^m$ = 1.36), broadly elliptic to elliptic, adaxially flattened, smooth, thin walled, hyaline, nonamyloid; contents guttulate; apiculus sublateral, usually cylindric.

Typification: No type was designated in the original description, but one specimen was cited. A packet from CUP shows a collection date matching almost perfectly that found in the original description. Since collections of this taxon are rare, I feel that this collection from CUP is probably the one cited by Kauffman. Therefore, this packet is recognized as the holotype (Lanjouw, 1966: Guide for the Determination of Types).

4. *Amanita cothurnata* Atk. 1900. Studies of American Fungi. Mushrooms: 66-69.

Lectotype (des. mihi): North Carolina - Blowing Rock, Watauga Co., 19. vii. - 10. ix. 1899, G. F. Atkinson 3715 "type specimen" (CUP).

Pileus approximately 4.5 cm diam, hemispherical to plane, moderately thin, margin striate; volval remnants as numerous, floccose patches. randomly distributed, frequently becoming thinner on margin. Lamellae free, crowded, rounded next to stipe, edges often finely ragged; lamellulae truncate. Stipe up to 4.5 x 0.7 cm, tapering upward, stuffed or hollow, basal bulb ovoid; annulus fragmentary approximately 1 cm from apex; volva as a close-fitting roll or forming thickened, irregular margin at apex of bulb.

Pileipellis of interwoven to subradial, gelatinized hyphae. Pileus trama composed of undifferentiated hyphae and inflated cells. Lamellar trama bilateral, hyphae undifferentiated, rarely exceeding 10 µ diam, inflated cells usually clavate to fusiform, terminal or occasionally very short, terminal chains; subhymenial hyphae ramose to slightly inflated; basidia 30-50 x 3-11 µ, (1-2)-4-sterigmate, rarely clamped. Hyphae of volva on pileus 3-8 µ diam, moderately branched, rarely clamped; inflated cells up to 51 x 125 µ, globose, subglobose, elliptic, ovoid, pyriform, clavate, single, terminal cells or more often randomly oriented, terminal chains of cells; hyphae of volva at base 3-7 µ diam, moderately branched, rarely clamped; inflated cells 51 x 160 µ, similar to those on pileus, arranged as terminal cells or terminal chains. Stipe trama hyphae 3-9 µ, diam; inflated cells up to 30 x 255 µ, slenderly clavate, terminal, longitudinally oriented. Hyphae of partial veil 2-6 µ diam, moderately branched, clamps not observed; inflated cells up to 32 x 94 µ, clavate to elliptic, usually terminal.

Spores (6.3)6.8-8.3(9.0) x 7.9-10.4(11.8) µ, ($\underline{E}$ = 1.19-1.40; $\underline{E}^m$ = 1.33), broadly elliptic to elliptic, adaxially flattened, smooth, hyaline, thin walled, nonamyloid; contents usually guttulate; apiculus sublateral, truncate-conic.

Typification: Atkinson did not designate a holotype, but cited one specimen and two other collection dates. Due to this uncertainty in citations a lectotype must be chosen. The collection selected is packet no. 3715, mentioned in the original description, and annotated as "type specimen." The fruit bodies are in good condition and adequately exhibit the characters of the taxon.

5. *Amanita crenulata* Pk. 1900. Bull. Torr. Bot. Club 27: 15.

Lectotype (des mihi): Massachusetts - Near Boston, 1899, Mrs. E. Blackford s.n.(NYS).

Pileus up to 4 cm diam, becoming convex or nearly plane, thin, margin striate; volval remnants as thin, floccose patches or slight warts. Lamellae crowded, with floccose-crenulate edges, reaching stipe; lamellulae truncate. Stipe up to 4.5 x 0.4-0.8 cm, tapering upward, stuffed, basal bulb globose to subglobose; no annular material remaining; volva remaining only as floccose-mealy remnants at apex of bulb.

Pileipellis of densely interwoven or subradial, gelatinized hyphae. Pileus trama hyphae undifferentiated and inconspicuous; inflated cells approximately up to 64 x 160 µ, clavate to irregularly elongate, terminal. Lamellar trama bilateral; hyphae undifferentiated; cells inflated; subhymenial hyphae ramose, clamps not observed; basidia 35-42 x 4-9.4 µ, 4-sterigmate, clamps not observed. Hyphae of volva on pileus 2-6.5 µ diam, sparsely to moderately branched, without clamps; gloeoplerous hyphae moderately abundant; inflated cells up to 51 x 75 µ, subglobose, ovoid, broadly elliptic, elliptic, fusiform, clavate, arranged mostly as randomly oriented, terminal chains, the terminal element usually broadly elliptic to ovoid: volva remnants at base very similar to those on pileus. Stipe trama hyphae undifferentiated and inconspicuous with terminal, clavate, longitudinally oriented cells, up to 32 x 200 µ.

Spores 7.0-8.7 x 7.9-8.7 µ, ($\underline{E}$ = 1.0-1.13; $\underline{E}^m$ = 1.04), globose to subglobose, smooth, hyaline, thin walled, nonamyloid; contents guttulate; apiculus sublateral, cylindric to truncate-conic.

Typification: Peck did not designate a holotype, but one specimen was cited. The information in the citation was vague and I could not find a collection that matched exactly. I do not feel, therefore, that this citation can be considered as the designation of a holotype. A collection was found, however, that matched the citation fairly closely, and it has been designated as the lectotype.

6. *Amanita frostiana* var. *pallidipes* Pk. 1899. Rep. N. Y. St. Mus. 53: 855.

Neotype (des mihi): New York - Port Jefferson, Suffolk Co., vii., C. H. Peck s.n.(NYS); mixed collection, specimens annotated.

Pileus approximately 2.5-4 cm diam, convex to plane, margin faintly striate; volval remnants as floccose patches or flattened warts. Lamellae free, crowded; lamellulae truncate. Stipe approximately 3.5-6 x 0.3-16 cm, tapering slightly upward, basal bulb ovoid; annulus fragmentary, 1.5-2 cm from apex of stipe; volva often extending above apex of bulb as slight, free margin.

Pileipellis of densely interwoven or subradial, gelatinized hyphae. Pileus trama composed of undifferentiated hyphae and inflated, elongate cells. Lamellar trama bilateral; hyphae undifferentiated; cells inflated; subhymenial hyphae ramose, clamps occasional; basidia 41-50 x 5-11.5 μ, 4-sterigmate, rarely clamped. Hyphae of volva on pileus up to 8 μ diam, moderately branched, rarely clamped; inflated cells up to 51 x 100 μ, ovoid, broadly elliptic, subglobose, elongate, elliptic, clavate, or fusiform, often as single, terminal cells or irregularly disposed to apico-basal chains of cells: hyphae of volva at base of stipe up to 7 μ diam, moderately branched, rarely clamped; inflated cells up to 40 x 100 μ, shapes similar to those on pileus but with a larger proportion of elongate cells. Stipe trama hyphae undifferentiated and relatively inconspicuous; inflated cells terminal, clavate, longitudinally oriented, up to 45 x 318 μ. Hyphae of partial veil up to 7 μ diam, moderately branched, rarely clamped; inflated cells rare, elongate, terminal, not exceeding 10 x 50 μ.

Spores (5.8)6.3-7.9(8.4) x (7.3)7.9-10.2 μ, ($\underline{E}$ = 1.13-1.46; E^m = 1.27), subglobose elliptic, adaxially flattened, smooth hyaline, thin walled, nonamyloid; contents guttulate; apiculus sublateral, cylindric to slightly truncate-conic.

Typification: There were no specimens originally cited, requiring designation of a neotype. The collection chosen is mixed, but includes fruit bodies exhibiting the characters of the original description. The two taxa can be separated on amyloidity of spores, those of the type fruit bodies of *Amanita frostiana* var. *pallidipes* exhibiting a negative reaction, the others reacting positively. Fruit bodies have been annotated appropriately.

7. *Amanita glabriceps* Pk. 1909. Bull. N. Y. St. Mus. 131: 18-19, pl. μ., fig. 1-4.

Lectotype (des mihi): New York - Coopers Plains, Steuben Co., vii., C. H. Peck s.n.(NYS).

Pileus approximately 7 cm diam, plano-convex to slightly depressed, thin, margin striate; no volval remnants on pileus. Lamellae free, crowded; lamellulae truncate. Stipe up to 0.9 x 14 cm, tapering upward, stuffed, floccose-squamulose, base clavate; annulus fragmentary, median; volva appressed with a slight, free ring of volval material above the free, margined collar.

Pileipellis of moderately dense interwoven to subradial, gelatinized hyphae. Pileus trama composed primarily of clavate to irregularly elongate, inflated cells; hyphae undifferentiated with clamps. Lamellar trama bilateral; hyphae undifferentiated; cells inflated; subhymenial hyphae ramose, occasionally clamped; basidia 39-50 x 4.5-9.4 μ, 4-sterigmate, no clamps observed. Hyphae of volva at base 2-6 μ diam, moderately branched, without clamps; inflated cells subglobose, broadly elliptic, ovoid, oblong-elliptic, elliptic, clavate, up to 45 x 64 μ. Stipe trama hyphae 3-8 μ diam, sparsely branched, rarely clamped; inflated cells terminal, clavate, longitudinally oriented, up to 35 x 240 μ. Hyphae of partial veil 3-6 μ diam, moderately branched, rarely clamped; inflated cells terminal, clavate, up to 25 x 180 μ.

Spores 6.3-7.9 x 7.9-9.4 μ, (E = 1.19-1.38; E^m = 1.28), broadly elliptic, elliptic, adaxially flattened, smooth, hyaline, nonamyloid; contents guttulate; apiculus sublateral, cylindric to truncate-conic.

Typification: In Peck's original description only two syntypes were cited, making mandatory the selection of a lectotype. Although both specimens cited were of comparable condition, the one collected by Peck was given preference.

8. *Agaricus monticulosus* Berk. & Curt, in Berk. 1853. Ann Mag. Nat. Hist. 12(2): 418.

≡ *Amanita monticulosa* (Berk & Curt.) Sacc. 1887. Syll. Fung. 5: 18.

Lectotype (des. mihi): South Carolina, ix. - xi., Curtis 2853 sheet II, packet II, right fruit body (K).

Pileus approximately 5.5 cm diam, convex to plano-convex, with a possible, slight umbo, areolate, margin not striate; volva remnants as angular or pyramidal warts in each areola, becoming more flocculent near margin of pileus. Stipe approximately 0.4 -

0.9 x 5 cm, tapering slightly upward, with subclavate to clavate basal bulb; volva fibrillose to fibrillose-scaly with subfloccose patches on margin of bulb.

Pileipellis of densely interwoven to subradial, gelatinized hyphae. Hyphae of volva on pileus 2-10 µ diam, mostly gloeoplerous, moderately branched, clamps not observed; inflated cells up to 35 x 80 µ, subglobose, elliptic, clavate, elongate, usually arranged as short, terminal, apico-basal chains, with some of the larger, elongate cells being terminal: hyphae of volva at base of stipe moderately branched, mostly gloeoplerous; inflated cells globose, subglobose, broadly elliptic, elongate, usually in terminal chains with broadest cells usually terminal. Stipe trama hyphae undifferentiated with terminal, elongate, longitudinally oriented cells. Basidia 42-47 x 4.5-11 µ, usually 4-sterigmate, no clamps observed.

Spores 7.0-8.0(9.0) x 9.8-11.2 µ, ($\underline{E}$ = 1.19-1.50; $\underline{E}^m$ = 1.35), broadly elliptic to elliptic, adaxially flattened, smooth, thin walled, hyaline, nonamyloid; contents guttulate; apiculus sublateral, truncate-conic.

Typification: In the original description no type was designated, but two specimens were cited. These syntypes are contained in three packets on one herbarium sheet at K. Collection no. 2829 is in one packet and no. 2853 is in two packets. The primary character used for the determination was the presence of pyramidal warts. Thus, the apico-basal arrangement of the chains of inflated cells in the volval remnants on the pileus separated the specimens on sheet II from those on sheets I and III. Also the specimen on sheet I had no spores. On sheet II the left-hand specimen is probably the same as the right-hand specimen, but because of its immaturity this is difficult to confirm. Therefore, the right-hand specimen on sheet II seems to be the best choice as the lectotype. This is in agreement with Bas (annotated specimen).

9. *Amanita multisquamosa* Pk. 1900. Rep. N. Y. St. Mus. 53: 840, pl. B, fig. 1-7.

Lectotype (des mihi): New York - Amagansett, Suffolk Co., vii., C. H. Peck s.n.(NYS).

Pileus approximately 4 cm diam, convex to plane, margin slightly striate; volval remnants as numerous, angular, erect warts, more closely spaced toward disc. Lamellae free, crowded: lamellulae truncate. Stipe approximately 5 x 0.3-0.6 cm, tapering slightly upward, stuffed; basal bulb ovoid; annulus fragmentary, approximately 2 cm from apex of stipe; volva as slight, free margin at apex of bulb, not inrolled.

Pileipellis a gelatinous layer with relatively little hyphal structure remaining. Pileus trama composed of undifferentiated hyphae and inflated, elongate cells. Lamellar trama bilateral; subhymenial hyphae ramose; basidia 40-47 x 4.5-11 μ, 4-sterigmate, no clamps observed. Hyphae of volva on pileus approximately 2-8 μ diam, moderately branched, occasionally clamped, with a significant number of gloeoplerous hyphae; inflated cells up to 51 x 76 μ, subglobose, broadly elliptic, ovoid, elliptic, oblong-elliptic, clavate, usually arranged in terminal, randomly oriented to apico-basal chains: hyphae of volva at base of stipe approximately 3-7 μ diam, moderately branched, with occasional clamps; inflated cells similar to those on pileus with a larger number of broadly shaped cells. Stipe trama hyphae up to 7 μ diam, moderately branched, clamped; inflated cells terminal, clavate, longitudinally oriented, up to 38 x 255 μ. Hyphae of partial veil up to 3-7 μ diam, moderately branched, clamped; inflated cells sparse, terminal, clavate, up to 20 x 130 μ.

Spores 7.0-8.7 x 8.7-11 μ, ($\underline{E}^m$ = 1.1-1.39; $\underline{E}^m$ = 1.22) subglobose to elliptic, often adaxially flattened, smooth, hyaline, nonamyloid, thin walled; contents guttulate; apiculus sublateral, truncate-conic.

Typification: Peck's original description contained no citation of specimens, but only three counties in which collections were made. The lectotype is from one of these, and has been chosen based on morphological similarities with the original description and in agreement with Bas (annotated specimen).

10. *Agaricus muscarius* Linnaeus. 1753. Species Plant. Ed. 1, 2: 1172.

≡ *Amanita muscaria* (Linnaeus per Fries) Hooker. 1821. Flora Scotica 2: 19.

Neotype (Jenkins & Petersen, 1976): Angermanland: Nordingra

Parish, Sweden. Summer, 1974, coll. R. H. Petersen 39847(TENN).

Fruit bodies subgregarious. Pileus 9-12 cm diam, convex to plano-convex, faintly to strongly striate on the margin, scarlet red "R" to grenadine red "R" over center, grenadine red "R" to orange chrome "R" toward the margin, viscid, glabrous; flesh apricot yellow "R" to cadmium "R" underneath pileipellis, white below; volval remnants as white to off-white floccose warts or patches, arranged randomly to nearly concentric rings, occasionally passing into thin, floccose material at margin. Lamellae crowded to moderately crowded, free and remote, broad to moderately broad, white to whitish, edges frequently minutely floccose; lamellulae concavely to convexly truncate. Stipe 6-12 x 0.8-1.8 cm, tapering upward with apex expanded, stuffed to hollow, white below, to pale maize yellow "R" to baryta yellow "R" above, fibrous to floccose-fibrillose scaly; basal bulb ovoid, whitish to pallid. Volva white to pale creamy-buff, ascending irregular rings of small to medium, floccose warts or patches, often leaving a shallow rim on upper portion of bulb, lower part of stipe often having several floccose, warty to recurved, scaly, ascending rings. Annulus apical to subapical, submembranous to floccose-felted, pendant, fragile, striate above, floccose below, edge often with small to medium, floccose chunks of volval material, often collapsing, lower surface white, upper surface maize yellow "R" to baryta yellow "R".

Filamentous hyphae of pileipellis 3-8 μ diam, interwoven to subradial, slightly to strongly gelatinized, hyaline to slightly yellowish in alkaline solution. Filamentous hyphae of pileus trama sparsely to moderately branched, up to 8 μ diam, clamped; inflated cells up to 46 x 220 μ, clavate, cylindric, or irregularly elongate, terminal or rarely in short, terminal chains. Lamellar trama bilateral with distinct mediostratum; filamentous hyphae 3-9 μ diam, moderately branched, clamped; inflated cells up to 30 x 120 μ, usually clavate to irregularly elongate, terminal or in short, terminal chains; subhymenium ramose, although at times cells slightly inflated and almost appearing cellular, hyphae occasionally clamped; basidia 38-58 x 3.9-11.2 μ, 4-sterigmate, occasionally clamped. Remnants of volva on pileus as dense to loose tissue of interwoven to erect filamentous hyphae, with terminal inflated cells or chains of inflated cells; filamentous hyphae 3-9 μ diam, abundant, moderately branched, clamped; inflated cells up to 47 x 63 μ, globose, subglobose, ovoid, broadly elliptic, elliptic, oblong-elliptic, clavate, cylindric, fusiform or astringo-cylindric: volval material at base of stipe very similar to that on pileus, with the cells generally slightly larger. Filamentous hyphae of stipe trama 2-6 μ diam, sparsely branched, usually clamped; inflated cells up to 62 x 455 μ, clavate, terminal, longitudinally oriented. Upper surface of partial veil composed of filamentous hyphae 2-6 μ diam, sparsely to moderately branched, clamped, occasional gloeoplerous segments, and inflated cells up to 12 x 88 μ, clavate to cylindric, terminal; lower surface exclusively of filamentous hyphae, similar to above, but often encrusted with yellowish, refractile material.

Spores 6.9-7.7 x 9.2-10 μ, ($\underline{E}$ = 1.30-1.48; $\underline{E}^m$ = 1.34), broadly elliptic to elliptic, adaxially flattened, thin walled, hyaline, white to pale cream in print, nonamyloid, guttulate; apiculus sublateral, cylindric to truncate-conic.

Typification: See Jenkins and Petersen, 1976.

11. *Agaricus muscarius* var. *alba* Pk. 1880. Rep. N. Y. St. Mus. 33: 44.

≡ *Amanita muscaria* var. *alba* (Pk.) Pk. 1893. Rep. N. Y. St. Mus. 46: 53.

Neotype (des. mihi): New York - Albany and Delmar, x. C. H. Peck s.n.(NYS).

Pileus approximately 4-9 μ diam, convex to plano-convex, relatively thin, margin striate; volval remnants as thin, floccose patches or small, angular warts, arranged in nearly concentric rings. Lamellae free to approximate, crowded; lamellulae truncate. Stipe up to 8 x 0.9 cm, tapering slightly upward, stuffed to hollow; basal bulb ovoid, up to 2 x 2.5 cm; annulus fragmentary; volva as irregular, floccose ringlets at apex of bulb and lower stipe.

Pileipellis of densely interwoven, gelatinized hyphae. Pileus trama composed of undifferentiated hyphae, 3-9 μ diam; inflated cells elongate. Lamellar trama bilateral; hyphae undifferentiated; cells inflated; subhymenial hyphae ramose, occasionally clamped; basidia 4-11.5 x 41-50 μ, usually 4-sterigmate, occasionally clamped. Hyphae of volva on pileus up to 8 μ diam, moderately branched, clamps occasional; inflated cells globose, subglobose, broadly elliptic, ovoid, elliptic, clavate, fusiform, up to 51 x 138 µ, arranged as random to apico-basal, terminal chains: hyphae of volva at base of stipe up to 8.5 µ diam, moderately branched, occasionally clamped, inflated cells very similar to those on pileus. Stipe trama hyphae undifferentiated and relatively inconspicuous with terminal, clavate, longitudinally oriented cells, up to 25 x 225 µ.

Spores 7.0-8.4 x 9.4-11.2 µ, ($\underline{E}$ = 1.29-1.45; $\underline{E}^m$ = 1.36), broadly elliptic to elliptic, adaxially flattened, smooth, hyaline, nonamyloid; contents guttulate; apiculus sublateral, cylindric.

Typification: Peck cited no specimens in the original description, thus requiring the designation of a neotype. The specimen above was chosen because of its proximity to Peck's primary collecting area, its acceptable condition, and the exhibition of morphological characters associated with the A. muscaria complex.

12. Agaricus muscarius var. minor Pk. 1869. Rep. N. Y. St. Mus. 23: 69.

≡ Amanita frostiana (Pk.) Sacc. 1887. Syll. Fung. 5: 14.

Neotype (des. mihi): New York - Croghan, Lewis Co., no date, C. H. Peck s.n.(NYS).

Pileus approximately 3 cm diam, convex or expanded, margin striate; volval remnants as small patches to small warts, more numerous over disc. Lamellae free, crowded; lamellulae truncate. Stipe approximately 5 x 0.3-1.5 cm, tapering slightly upward, stuffed, bulbous at base; annulus fragmentary, approximately 1.5 cm from stipe apex; volva extending above bulb as slight margin, with narrow, ascending rings of floccose material below margin of bulb.

Pileipellis of densely interwoven to subradial, gelatinized hyphae. Pileus trama of undifferentiated hyphae with inflated cells. Lamellar trama bilateral; hyphae undifferentiated; cells inflated; subhymenial hyphae ramose, clamps not observed; basidia 40-50 x 4.5-11 µ, 4-sterigmate, clamp connections rare. Hyphae of volva on pileus 3-7 µ diam, scarcely to moderately branched, clamped; inflated cells globose, subglobose, broadly elliptic, ovoid, up to 57 x 76 µ, with clavate, fusiform, oblong-elliptic, astringo-elliptic, up to 38 x 160 μ, arranged as irregular or apico-basal, terminal chains; hyphae of volva at base of stipe 3-9 μ diam, moderately branched, frequently clamped; inflated cells very similar to those above. Stipe trama hyphae undifferentiated and inconspicuous with terminal, oblong-elliptic to clavate, longitudinally oriented, inflated cells, up to 35 x 240 μ. Hyphae of partial veil 3-8 μ diam, moderately branched, clamped, with occasional, terminal, inflated cells up to 20 x 160 μ.

Spores 7.9-8.7 x 7.9-8.7 μ, ($\underline{E}$ = 1.0-1.0; $\underline{E}^m$ = 1.01), globose to subglobose, smooth, hyaline, nonamyloid, thin walled; contents guttulate; apiculus sublateral, truncate-conic.

Typification: Peck did not cite any specimens in the original description, forcing the selection of a neotype. The collection chosen as type is mixed, containing fruit bodies of two morphologically similar taxa. When Peck changed the rank of the taxon he emended the original description by adding the character of globose spore shape. This enables division of this collection into fruit bodies with globose spores (A. *frostiana*) and those with elliptic spores (presumably A. *flavoconia*). In addition the globose spores of A. *frostiana* are nonamyloid while those of the other taxon are amyloid.

13. *Agaricus nivalis* Pk. 1880. Rep. N. Y. St. Mus. 33: 48.
≡ *Amanita nivalis* (Pk.) Lloyd. 1898. Volvae: 9.

Neotype (des. mihi): New York - Worcester, Otsego Co., no date, C. H. Peck s.n.(NYS).

Pileus approximately 4.5-5 cm diam, plane, thin; margin striate; no volval remnants on pileus. Lamellae barely free, crowded; lamellulae truncate. Stipe approximately 10 x 0.6 cm, tapering slightly upward, base subglobose to ovoid; annulus none; volva delicate, floccose, at apex of bulb forming a fragile rim-like structure or leaving fragments on lower stipe.

Pileipellis a layer of interwoven, gelatinized hyphae. Hyphae of pileus trama relatively slender and moderately branched; inflated cells clavate to irregularly elongate, up to 32 x 130 μ. Lamellar trama bilateral; filamentous hyphae undifferentiated; inflated cells oblong-elliptic to clavate, up to 24 x 110 μ, terminal or in very short, terminal chains; subhymenial hyphae ramose, rarely clamped; basidia 40-47 x 4.7-11 μ, 4-sterigmate, rarely clamped. Filamentous hyphae of volva at base of stipe up to 7 μ diam, sparsely branched, without clamps; inflated cells up to 25 x 125 μ, subglobose, broadly elliptic, ovoid, oblong-elliptic, clavate, usually as irregularly disposed, terminal chains. Stipe trama filamentous hyphae up to 6 μ diam, sparsely branched, without clamps; inflated cells terminal, clavate, longitudianlly oriented, up to 32 x 380 μ.

Spores 6.3-7.9 x 7.0-9.4 μ, (E = 1.11-1.38; E^m = 1.20), subglobose to elliptic, often adaxially flattened, smooth, hyaline, thin walled, nonamyloid; contents guttulate; apiculus sublateral, cylindric.

Typification: In the original description Peck cited no specimens, thereby forcing the selection of a neotype. He did, however, mention in his discussion three counties in which he had collected the fungus. Based on the similarity of morphological characters of these specimens to the original description, the neotype has been selected from collections from these locations.

14. *Venenarius pantherinoides* Murrill. 1912. Mycologia 4: 242.
≡ *Amanita pantherinoides* (Murr.) Sacc. 1925. Syll. Fung. 13: 2.

Holotype: Washington - South slope in woods near Seattle, 20. x. - 1. xi. 1911, W. A. Murrill 399(NY).

Pileus up to 4.5 cm diam, convex to plane, relatively thin, margin not striate; volva distributed as thin, floccose patches. Lamellae free, crowded; lamellulae truncate. Stipe up to 7 x 0.7 cm, tapering slightly upward, stuffed, basal bulb ovoid; annular remnants approximately 2 cm from apex of stipe; volva as small, free margin and occasional floccose material at apex of bulb.

Pileipellis of densely interwoven, gelatinized hyphae. Hyphae of pileus trama undifferentiated; inflated cells up to 32 x 160 μ, clavate to irregularly elongate; subhymenial hyphae ramose to slightly inflated-ramose, rarely clamped; basidia 39-47 x 4.5-11 μ, 4-sterigmate, clamps not observed. Hyphae of volva on pileus up to 8 μ diam, scarcely to moderately branched, clamps not observed; inflated cells up to 58 x 83 μ, subglobose, ovoid, broadly elliptic, elliptic, oblong-elliptic, clavate, usually arranged as randomly oriented, terminal chains: hyphae of volva at base of stipe up to 7 μ diam, moderately branched; clamps not observed; inflated cells up to 38 x 105 μ, primarily clavate to oblong-elliptic, with a lesser number broadly elliptic to ovoid, arranged as terminal cells or short, terminal chains. Stipe trama hyphae undifferentiated and inconspicuous with terminal, clavate, longitudinally oriented cells, up to 32 x 286 μ. Hyphae of partial veil 1.5-6 μ diam, moderately branched, rarely clamped; inflated cells 25 x 130 μ, clavate to elliptic, usually terminal.

Spores 6.3-7.9 x 9.4-11.0 μ, (E = 1.39-1.62; E^m = 1.59), elliptic to elongate, often adaxially flattened, smooth, hyaline, thin walled, nonamyloid; contents guttulate; apiculus sublateral, usually cylindric.

15. *Amanitopsis parcivolvata* Pk. 1900. Bull. Torr. Bot. Club 27(12): 610.

≡ *Amanita parcivolvata* (Pk.) Gilb. 1941. Iconogr. Mycol. 27(2): 226.

Lectotype (des. mihi): North Carolina - Skyland, Henderson Co., vii., Miss Mary L. Wilson s.n.(NYS).

Pileus approximately 3 cm diam, convex to plane, flesh thin, margin striate; no volval remnants remaining. Lamellae free, crowded; lamellulae truncate. Stipe approximately 3 x 0.2-0.4 cm, tapering slightly upward, stuffed, base ovoid; volval remnants as sparse, very fine floccose material at top of basal bulb.

Pileipellis of densely interwoven, gelatinized hyphae. Pileus trama of undifferentiated hyphae and elongate, inflated cells. Lamellar trama bilateral; hyphae approximately 3-6 μ diam, moderately branched, clamped; inflated cells up to 25 x 100 μ, elongate, terminal or as short, terminal chains; subhymenial hyphae ramose, clamped; basidia 40-47 x 4.5-12.6 μ, 4-sterigmate, clamps not observed. Hyphae of volva at base of stipe very sparse, approximately 2-6 μ diam, moderately branched, rarely clamped; inflated cells up to 64 x 70 μ, globose, subglobose, ovoid, broadly elliptic, elliptic, clavate, usually arranged as terminal, randomly oriented chains. Stipe trama hyphae undifferentiated and inconspicuous; inflated cells terminal, clavate to oblong-elliptic cells, longitudinally oriented, 64 x 222 μ.

Spores 6.3-7.9 x 11.0-11.8 μ, ($\underline{E}$ = 1.39-1.75; $\underline{E}^m$ = 1.52), elliptic to elongate, often adaxially flattened, hyaline, non-amyloid, thin walled contents guttulate; apiculus sublateral, cylindric to truncate-conic.

Typification: In the original description two syntypes were cited. Although a lectotype should ideally be a specimen collected by the original author, neither of the syntypes was collected by Peck. The specimen in the best condition was, therefore, selected.

16. *Venenarius praegemmatus* Murrill. 1912. Mycologia 4: 243.
≡ *Amanita praegemmata* (Murr.) Sacc. 1925. Syll. Fung. 13: 13.

Holotype: Washington - On sandy soil in open woods near Seattle, 20. x. - 1. xi. 1911, W. A. Murrill 247(NY).

Pileus approximately 4 cm diam, convex to plano-convex, margin not striate; volval remnants as floccose-fibrillose patches or occasionally angular warts covering most of pileus. Lamellae free, crowded; lamellulae truncate. Stipe approximately 4 x 0.3-0.5 cm, tapering slightly upward, stuffed, bulbous at base, annular remains very slight, approximately 1 cm from apex of stipe; volva appressed, extending only slightly above bulb as shallow, free margin.

Pileipellis of densely interwoven to subradial, gelatinized hyphae. Lamellar trama bilateral, with hyphae 2-7 μ diam, moderately branched, rarely clamped; inflated cells elongate, terminal or short, terminal chains; subhymenial hyphae ramose, occasionally clamped; basidia 39-47 x 4.5-12.5 μ, 4-sterigmate, clamps occasional. Remnants of volva on pileus a fairly loose tissue of irregularly disposed to occasionally apico-basal, terminal chains of globose, subglobose, ovoid, broadly elliptic, inflated cells up to 45 x 64 μ, with clavate, elliptic, and oblong-elliptic cells up to 38 x 115 μ; hyphae 3-8 μ diam, sparsely to moderately branched, rarely clamped: inflated cells of volva at base of stipe up to 31 x 127 μ, primarily elongate to clavate, less frequently very small, broadly elliptic to ovoid, terminal or in short, terminal chains; hyphae 3-7 μ diam, moderately branched, rarely clamped. Stipe trama cells up to 35 x 220 μ, terminal, clavate, longitudinally oriented. Partial veil hyphae

3-7 μ diam, moderately branched, rarely clamped, occasionally terminating in an inflated, clavate cell, up to 20 x 125 μ.

Spores 6.3-7.0 x 8.7-9.4 μ, ($\underline{E}$ = 1.34-1.49; $\underline{E}^m$ = 1.43), elliptic, adaxially flattened, smooth, thin walled, hyaline, nonamyloid; contents guttulate; apiculus sublateral, cylindric to truncate-conic.

17. *Agaricus russuloides* Pk. 1873. Bull. Buff. Soc. Nat. Sci. 1(2): 41.

≡ *Amanita russuloides* (Pk.) Sacc. 1887. Syll. Fung. 5: 13.

Holotype: New York - Greenbush, Rensselaer Co., no date, C. H. Peck s.n.(NYS).

Pileus approximately 3.5 cm diam, convex to plano-convex, margin striate; volval remnants as a few widely scattered, floccose patches. Lamellae crowded, free but connected to stipe by a floccose line; lamellulae truncate. Stipe approximately 3.5 x 0.2-0.5 cm, tapering slightly upward, stuffed, smooth, bulbous at base; no annulus; volva as a slight, free limb at the apex of the bulb with occasional floccose patches on lower stem.

Pileipellis of densely interwoven to subradial, gelatinized hyphae. Lamellar trama bilateral; hyphae 3-8 μ diam, moderately branched, clamps not observed; inflated cells up to 25 x 130 μ, mostly clavate and irregularly elongate; subhymenial hyphae ramose, clamps not observed; basidia 39-50 x 4.1-12 μ, 4-sterigmate, clamps rarely observed. Remnants of volva on pileus a loose to fairly dense tissue of apico-basal to irregularly disposed, terminal chains of clavate, elliptic, oblong-elliptic, astringo-cylindric inflated cells; cells up to 32 x 110 μ, with broadly elliptic and ovoid cells up to 40 x 64 μ; hyphae of volva 4-8 μ diam, moderately branched, clamps not observed: inflated cells of basal volva very similar to those on pileus with elliptic and ovoid cells larger, usually arranged in irregularly disposed, terminal chains; filamentous hyphae 3-8 μ diam, moderately branched, rarely clamped. Stipe trama hyphae up to 8 μ diam, sparsely branched, clamps rare; inflated cells up to 32 x 255 μ, clavate, terminal, longitudinally oriented.

Spores 6.3-7.0 x 8.7-10.2 μ, ($\underline{E}$ = 1.24-1.49; $\underline{E}^m$ = 1.40), broadly elliptic to elliptic, adaxially flattened, thin walled, smooth, hyaline, nonamyloid; contents guttulate; apiculus sublateral, cylindric.

Typification: The specimen citation in the original description is very incomplete and under ordinary circumstances would not suffice as a citation. However, this taxon appears to be rare and Peck (1905) later stated that he had made no additional collections at Greenbush. Under these conditions I feel that the citation justifies the matching packet at NYS as a holotype (Lanjouw, 1966; Guide for the Determination of Types).

18. *Amanita velatipes* Atk. 1900. Studies of American Fungi. Mushrooms: 63-66, figs. 64-67.

Neotype (des. mihi): New York - Beech woods, Cayuga Lake Basin, 28. vii. 1897, Hasselbring 3167(CUP).

Pileus approximately 12.5 cm diam, plano-convex to plane, margin strongly striate; volval remnants as angular warts or patches whose margins are often reflexed. Lamellae free, crowded; lamellulae truncate. Stipe approximately 16 x 0.9-1.3 cm, tapering slightly upward, stuffed, ovoid to subradicate at base; annular remains few; volva as ring of floccose material about 1 cm above bulb and with slight deposits of floccose material on apex of bulb.

Pileipellis thin, interwoven to subradial, gelatinized hyphae. Hyphae of pileus trama undifferentiated; inflated cells 31 x 222 µ, clavate to irregularly elongate. Lamellar trama bilateral; hyphae undifferentiated; cells inflated; subhymenial hyphae ramose, clamped; basidia 40-47 x 4-9.4 µ, 4-sterigmate, occasionally clamped. Hyphae of volva on pileus 3-9 µ diam, moderately branched, rarely clamped; inflated cells up to 44 x 63 µ, subglobose, ovoid, broadly elliptic, oblong-elliptic, irregularly elongate, usually arranged in randomly oriented to apico-basal, terminal chains: hyphae of volva at base of stipe 3-8 µ diam, moderately branched, rarely clamped, gloeoplerous hyphae moderately abundant; inflated cells few, up to 50 x 130 µ, subglobose, ovoid, pyriform, elliptic, clavate, often terminal or in short, terminal chains. Stipe trama hyphae 3-6.5 µ diam, sparsely branched, rarely clamped; inflated cells up to 38 x 320 µ, clavate, terminal, longitudinally oriented. Hyphae of partial veil 2-6 µ diam, moderately branched, clamped, most hyphal tips terminated by an inflated, narrowly clavate cell, up to 13 x 95 μ.

Spores 5.5-6.3 x 7.9-9.4 μ, ($\underline{E}$ = 1.25-1.71; $\underline{E}^m$ = 1.42), broadly elliptic to elongate, often adaxially flattened, smooth, hyaline, nonamyloid, thin walled; contents guttulate; apiculus, sublateral, cylindric.

Typification: Because no specimens were cited in the original description, a neotype has been chosen. It agrees with the original description and was collected in the same general area originally cited.

19. *Venenarius wellsii* Murr. 1920. Mycologia 12: 291-292.
≡ *Amanita wellsii* (Murr.) Sacc. 1925. Syll. Fung. 13: 2-3.

Holotype: New Hampshire - Springfield, "about" 1. ix. 1917, W. A. Murrill s.n.(NY).

Pileus approximately 5.5 cm diam, convex to plano-convex, margin not striate; volval remnants scarce, minimal amount of pulverulent material remaining. Lamellae free, crowded; lamellulae truncate. Stipe approximately 10 x 0.4-0.9 cm, tapering slightly upward, stuffed, base subglobose; annulus not present; volva present only as sparsely scattered, pulverulent material.

Hyphae of pileus trama 4-10 μ diam, moderately branched, clamps rare. Lamellar trama bilateral; hyphae 3-9 μ diam, moderately branched, occasionally clamped; inflated cells up to 25 x 150 μ, clavate to irregularly elongate; subhymenial hyphae ramose to slightly inflated-ramose; basidia 42-47 x 4.5-9.5 μ, 4-sterigmate, clamps not observed. Hyphae of volva on pileus 3-8 μ diam, moderately branched, rarely clamped; inflated cells up to 25 x 110 μ, often elliptic, clavate, fusiform, irregularly elongate, less frequently broadly elliptic to ovoid, up to 42 x 80 μ, usually arranged as randomly oriented, terminal chains: hyphae of volva at base of stipe 3-9 μ diam, moderately branched, occasionally clamped. Stipe trama hyphae 3-7 μ diam, moderately branched, clamps not observed; inflated cells up to 38 x 470 μ, clavate, terminal, longitudinally oriented.

Spores 6.3-7.9 x 11.0-12.6 μ, ($\underline{E}$ = 1.48-2.0; $\underline{E}^m$ = 1.63), elliptic to cylindric, adaxially flattened, smooth, hyaline, nonamyloid, thin walled; contents guttulate; apiculus sublateral, cylindric.

BIBLIOGRAPHY

Atkinson, G. F. 1897. Some Fungi From Alabama Bull. Cornell Univ. III(1): 24-26.

_____. 1900. Studies of American Fungi. Mushrooms Edible, Poisonous, etc., 2nd Ed. (Reprint 1961, New York).

_____. 1902. Some New Species of Fungi. Jour. Mycol. 8: 110-119.

_____. 1909. A Remarkable Amanita. Bot. Gaz. 48(4): 283-293.

_____. 1914. The Development of *Amanitopsis vaginata*. Annls. Mycol. 12: 369-392.

Bary, A. de. 1866. Morphologie und Physiologie der Pilze, Flechten und Myxomyceton. In Handb. Physiol. Bot. 2, I Abt. Leipzig.

Bas, C. 1969. Morphology and Subdivision of *Amanita* and a Monograph on its Section *Lepidella*. Persoonia 5(4): 285-579.

_____. 1975. A Comparison of *Torrendia* (Gasteromycetes) with *Amanita* (Agaricales). Studies on Higher Fungi. Beih. Nova Hedwigia 51: 53-61.

Beardslee, H. C. 1902. Notes on *Amanitas* of the Southern Appalachians. Mycological Writings 1: 2-8.

_____. 1908. The *Amanitas* of North Carolina. Jour. Elish. Mitch. Sci. Soc. 24(4): 115-124.

_____. 1914. Notes on a Few Asheville Fungi. Mycologia 6: 88-92

_____. 1934. New and Interesting Fungi. Mycologia 26: 253-260.

Benedict, R. G., V. E. Tyler and L. R. Brady. 1966. Chemotaxonomic Significance of Isoxazole Derivatives in *Amanita*

Species. Llyodia 29(4): 333-342.

Berkeley, M. J. and M. A. Curtis. 1849. North and South Carolina Fungi. Hook. Jour. Bot. 1: 97-98.

Boudier, J. L. E. 1866. Les Champignons au Point de Vue de leurs Caracteres Usuels, Chimiques et Toxologiques. Paris.

Braddy, R. A. 1970. The Genus *Amanita* in North Carolina. Thesis, North Carolina State University.

Breckon, G. J. 1968. A Taxonomic Survey of the Genus *Amanita* in Northern California. Thesis, San Francisco State University.

Buck, R. W. 1965. Poisoning by *Amanita crenulata*. New England Jour. Medic. 272: 475-476.

_____. 1969. Nycetism. New England Jour. Medic. 280: 1363.

Chilton, W. S. and J. Ott. 1976. Toxic Metabolites of *Amanita pantherina*, A. *cothurnata*, A. *muscaria* and other *Amanita* species. Lloydia 39(2,3): 150-157.

Coker, W. C. 1917. The *Amanitas* of the Eastern United States. Jour. Elish. Mitch. Sci. Soc. 33(1,2): 1-88.

Cook. K. F. 1954. The Toxicity of Certain Species of *Amanita* in Guinea Pigs. Mycologia 46: 24-31.

Corner, E. J. H. 1932. A Fomes with Two Systems of Hyphae. Trans. Brit. Mycol. Soc. 17: 51.

_____. 1947. Variation in the Size and Shape of Spores, Basidia, and Cystidia in Basidiomycetes. New Phytologist 46: 195-228.

_____. and C. Bas. 1962. The Genus *Amanita* in Singapore and Malaya. Persoonia 2: 241-304.

Dearness, J. 1935. Mushroom Poisoning Due to *Amanita cothurnata*. Mycologia 27: 85-86.

Donk, M. A. 1949. Nomenclatural Notes on Generic Names of

Agarics (Fungi: Agaricales). Bull. Bot. Gdns. Buitenzorg III 18: 271-402.

Earle, F. S. 1909. The Genera of North American Gill Fungi. Bull. N. Y. Bot. Gdn. 5: 373-451.

Eugster, C. H., G. F. R. Muller and R. Good. 1965. Wirkstoffe aus *Amanita muscaria*: Ibotensaeure and Muscazon. Tetrahedron Letters 23: 1813-1815.

Fries, E. M. 1815. Observationes Mycologicae I. Havniae.

_____. 1821. Systema Mycologicum I. Lundae.

_____. 1838. Epicrisis Systematis Mycologici. Upsaliae.

Gilbert, E. J. 1930. Notules sur les *Amanites*. Bull. Soc. Mycol. France 45: 157-176.

_____. 1940. *Amanitaceae* I. Bresadola, Iconogr. Mycol. 27(1): 1-200.

_____. 1941a. Idem 2 & 3. Bresadola, Iconogr. Mycol. 27(2,3): 201-427.

_____. 1941b. Notules sur les *Amanites*. Suppl.: 1-23.

_____. and R. Kuhner. 1928. Recherches sur les Spores des *Amanites*. Bull. Soc. Mycol. France 44: 149-154.

Gilbertson, R. L. 1966. A Case of Poisoning by a Mushroom in the *Amanita pantherina* complex. Mycologia 58: 961-962.

Good, R., G. F. R. Muller and C. H. Eugster. 1965. Isolierung und Charakterisierung von Pramuscimol und Muscazon aus *Amanita muscaria* (L. ex Fr.) Hook. Helv. Chim. Acta 48: 927-962.

Gray, S. F. 1821. A Natural Arrangement of British Plants. London.

Hacskaylo, E. 1971. The Role of Mycorrhizal Associations in the Evolution of the Higher Basidiomycetes. Evolution of the Higher Basidiomycetes. University of Tennessee, Knoxville.

Hatch, A. B. and C. T. Hatch. 1933. Some Hymenomycetes Forming Ectotrophic Mycorrhizae with *Pinus strobus*. Jour. Arnold Arbor. 14: 324-334.

Heim, R. 1963. Les Champignons Toxiques et Hallucinogenes. Paris.

_____. 1965. Un Probleme a Eclaircir: celui de la Tue-Mouche. Rev. Mycol. 30(4): 294-298.

Hesler, L. R. 1930. Some *Amanitas* of Eastern Tennessee. Univ. Tenn. Record Ext. Serv. 1: 33-53.

Hoffman, H. 1861. Icones Analyticae Fungorum. Geissen.

Hooker, W. J. 1821. Flora Scotica. London.

Hotson, J. W. 1936. The *Amanitae* of Washington. Mycologia 28: 63-76.

Imai, S. 1938. Studies on the Agaricaceae of Hokkaido. I. Jour. Dac. Agri. Hokk. Imper. Univ. 43: 1-31.

Jenkins, D. T. and R. H. Petersen. 1976. A Neotype Specimen for *Amanita muscaria*. Mycologia 68(3): 463-469.

Kornerup, A. and J. H. Wanscher. 1967. Methuen Handbook of Color. 2nd Ed. London.

Kotlaba, F. and Z. Pouzar. 1964. Preliminary Results on the Staining of Spores and Other Structures of Monobasidiomycetes in Cotton Blue and Its Importance for Taxonomy. Feddes Repear. 69: 131-142.

Krieger, L. C. C. 1921. Is *Amanita pantherina* Edible or Poisonous? Mycologia 13: 270-271.

_____. 1936. The Mushroom Handbook. New York.

Kuntze, C. E. O. 1891. Rev. Gen. Plant. II: 867-868. Leipzig.

Lange, J. E. 1934. Mycofloristic Impressions of a European Mycologist in America. Mycologia 26: 1-12.

Lanjouw, J. 1966. International Code of Botanical Nomenclature.

Utrecht.

Lanjouw, J. and F. A. Stafleu. 1964. Index Herbariorum, Part I. The Herbaria of the World. Regn. Veget. 31: 1-251.

Linnaeus, C. 1737. Genera Plantarum. Leiden.

Maire, R. 1913. Etudes Mycologiques. Annales Mycologici 11: 331-358.

Micheli, P. A. 1729. Nova Plantarum Genera. Florentiae.

Muller, G. F. R. and C. H. Eugster. 1965. Muscimol, ein Pharmakodynamisch Wirksamer Stoff aus *Amanita muscaria*. Helv. Chim. Acta 48: 910-926.

Murrill, W. A. 1912. Agaricaceae of the Pacific Coast. Mycologia 4: 262.

_____. 1912. New Combinations for Tropical Agarics. Mycologia 4: 332.

_____. 1913. The *Amanitas* of Eastern North America. Mycologia 5: 83.

_____. 1916. Edible and Poisonous Mushrooms. New York.

_____. 1920. Notes and Brief Articles. Mycologia 12: 291-292.

Nakamura, N. 1965. A Survey of *Amanita* in Western Washington. Thesis, University of Washington.

Onda, M., H. Fukushima and M. Akagawa. 1964. A Flyicidal Constituent of *Amanita pantherina* (DC) Fr. Chem. Pharm. Bull. (Tokyo) 12: 751.

Paulet, J. J. 1778. Mem. Soc. Roy. Medic. pl. 15, fig. 3.

_____. and J. H. Levielle. 1855. Iconographie des Champignons. pl. 158, fig. 3.

Peck, C. H. 1869. Agaricini. Rep. N. Y. St. Bot. 23: 69.

_____. 1880. New York Species of *Amanita*. Rep. N. Y. St. Mus. 33: 44.

_____. 1900. New Species of Fungi. Bull. Tor. Bot. Club 27: 15.

_____. 1905. Remarks and Observations. Rep. N. Y. St. Mus. 105: 30.

Persoon, C. H. 1797. Tentamen Dispositionis Methodicae Fungorum. Lipsiae.

_____. 1799. Observationes Mycologicae. Lipsiae.

Reijnders. A. F. M. 1963. Les Problemes du Developpement des Carpophores des Agaricales et de Quelques Groupes Voisins. Den Haag.

Ridgeway, R. 1912. Color Standards and Nomenclature. Washington, D. C.

Roze, E. 1876. Essai d'une Nouvelle Classifications des Agaricacees. Bull. Soc. Bot. France 23: 45-54.

Saccardo, P. A. 1925. Sylloge Fungorum 23: 2-3.

Seaver, F. J. and P. F. Shope. 1935. New or Noteworthy Basidiomycetes from the Central Rocky Moutain Region. Mycologia 27: 642-651.

Singer, R. 1955. Type Studies on Basidiomycetes. VIII. Sydowia 9: 367-431.

_____. 1962. The Agaricales in Modern Taxonomy. 2nd Ed. Weinheim.

Smith, A. H. 1958. The Mushroom Hunter's Field Guide. 7th Ed. 1971 Univ. Mich. Press.

_____. 1971. Taxonomy of Ectomycorrhizae-forming Fungi. In Mycorrhizae-Proceedings of the First North American Conference on Mycorrhizae. Washington.

_____. and L. R. Hesler. 1938. Notes on Agarics from Tennessee and North Carolina. Jour. Elish. Mitch. Sci.

Soc. 54(2): 262-269.

Takemoto, T., T. Nakajima and P. Sakuma. Isolation of a Flyicidal Constituent "ibotenic acid" from *Amanita muscaria* and *A. pantherina.* Yakugaku Zasshi 84: 1233-1234.

Tyler, V. E., Jr. 1958. Pilzatropine, the Ambiguous Alkaloid, Amer. Jour. Pharm. 130: 264-269.

_____. 1962. Mushrooms, Pharmacognosy, and Creative Research. Jour. Pharm. 3(1): 105-119.

Wasson, R. G. 1968. Soma: Divine Mushroom of Immortality. New York.

Zeller, S. M. 1933. New or Noteworthy Agarics from Oregon. Mycologia 25: 376-391.

Plate 1. *Amanita farinosa.* DTJ 1239.

Plate 2. *Amanita frostiana.* DTJ 303.

Plate 3. *Amanita gemmata*. DTJ 1295.

Plate 4. *Amanita muscaria* var. *muscaria*. TENN 39847.

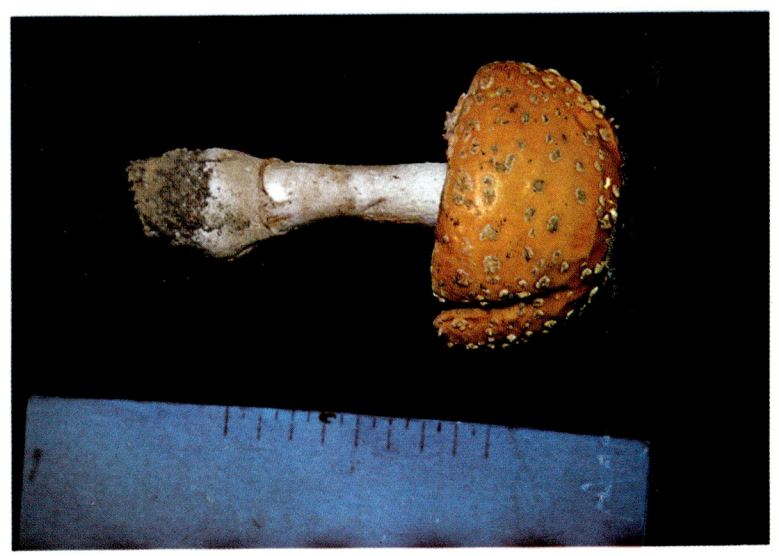

Plate 5. *Amanita muscaria* var. *formosa*. DTJ 439.

Plate 6. *Amanita muscaria* var. *flavivolvata*. DTJ 1351.

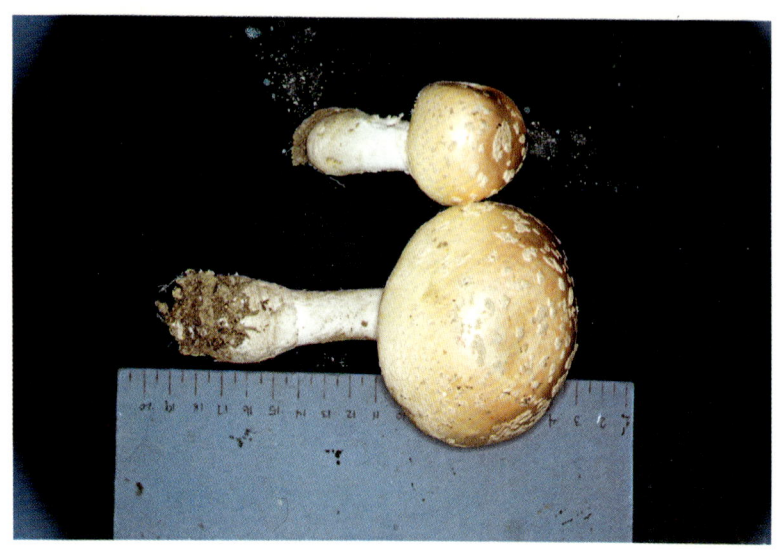

Plate 7. Amanita muscaria var. persicina. DTJ 671.

Plate 8. Amanita pantherina var. pantherina. DTJ 1331.

Plate 9. Amanita pantherina var. multisquamosa. DTJ 1290.

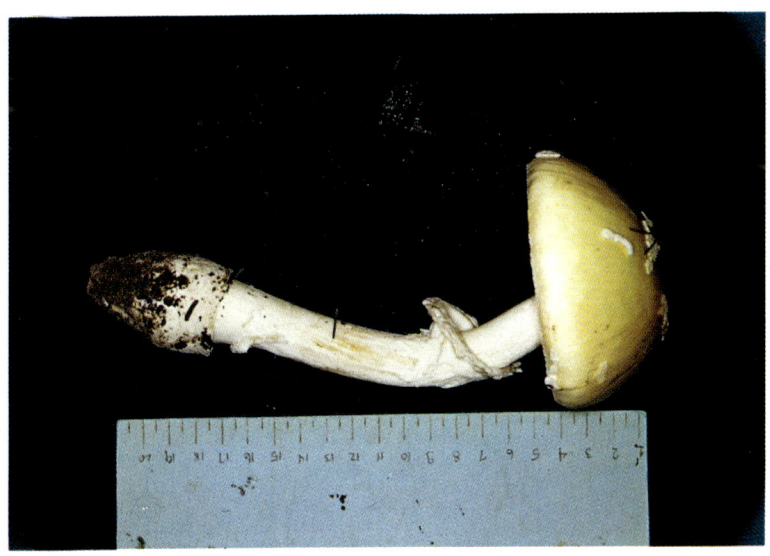

Plate 10. Amanita pantherina var. velatipes. DTJ 674.

Plate 11. *Amanita parcivolvata*. DTJ 622.

Plate 12. *Amanita wellsii*.

Plate 13.   Fruit body development
            Series of developing fruit bodies
            Amanita muscaria var. *flavivolvata*

Plate 14.   Fruit body development
            Series of developing fruit bodies
            Amanita muscaris var. *flavivolvata*

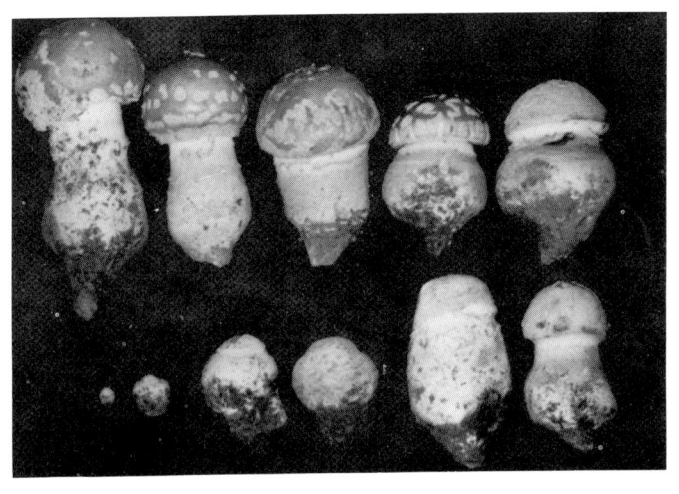

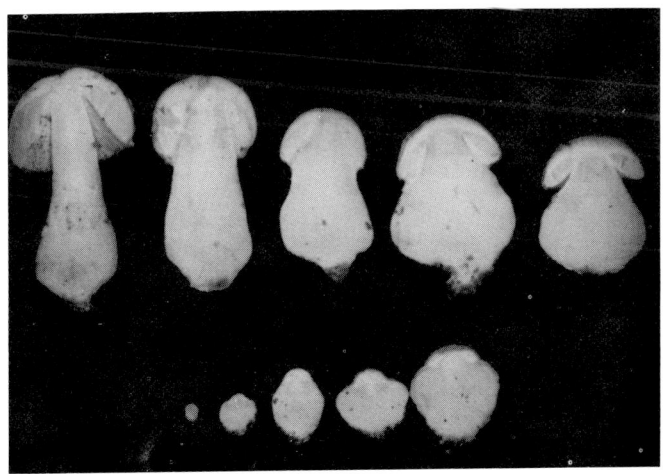

13
14

Plate 15. Gelatinous pileipellis

Plate 16. Pileus trama
 Amanita pantherina var. multisquamosa

Plate 17. Bilateral gill trama

Plate 18. Subhymenium with clamps
 Amanita muscaria var. flavivolvata

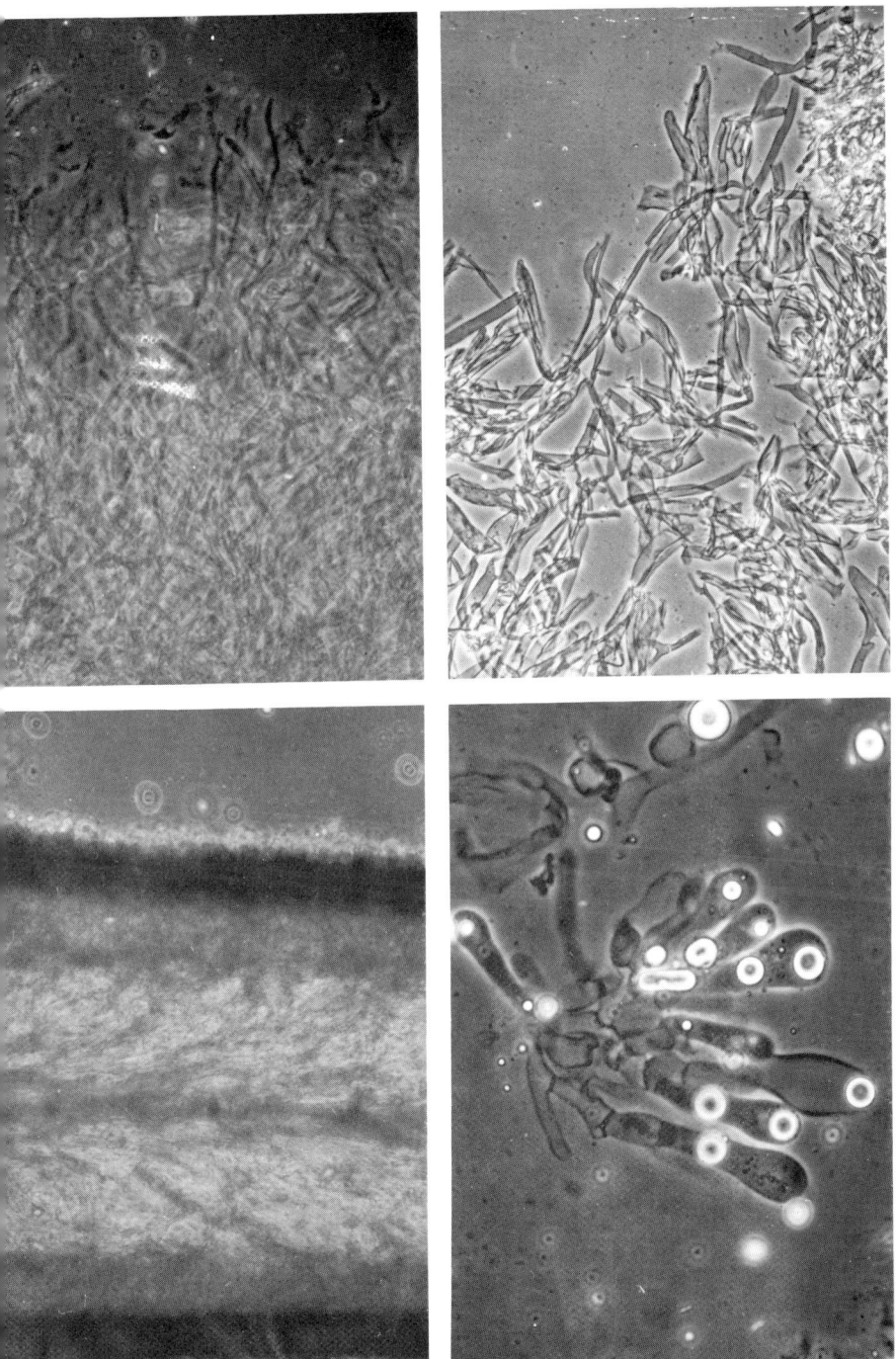

Plate 19. Basidia with clamps
           Amanita muscaria var. *flavivolvata*

Plate 20. Range of spore shapes
           within Section *Amanita*
           Globose - *Amanita frostiana*
           Broadly elliptic - *Amanita muscaria*
           Elongate - *Amanita wellsii*

Plate 21. Stipe trama

Plate 22. Partial veil
           Amanita pantherina var. *multisquamosa*

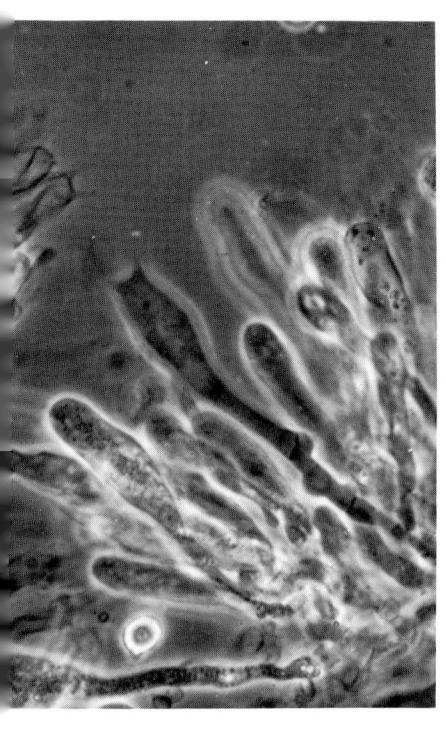
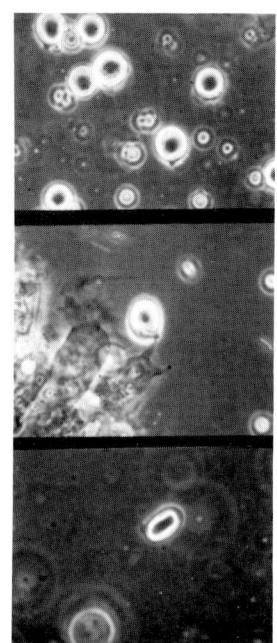
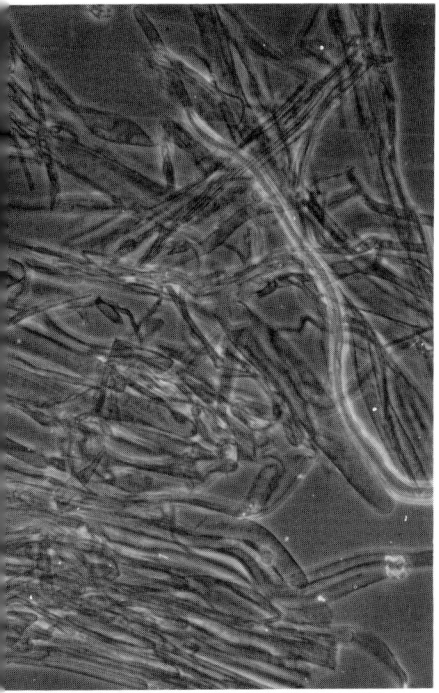
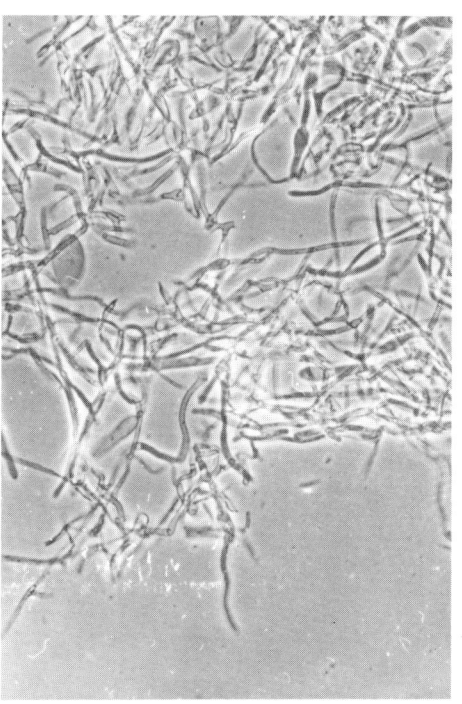

Plate 23. Volva of *Amanita farinosa*

Plate 24. Volva of *Amanita frostiana*

Plate 25. Volva of *Amanita gemmata*

Plate 26. Volva of *Amanita muscaria* var. *muscaria*

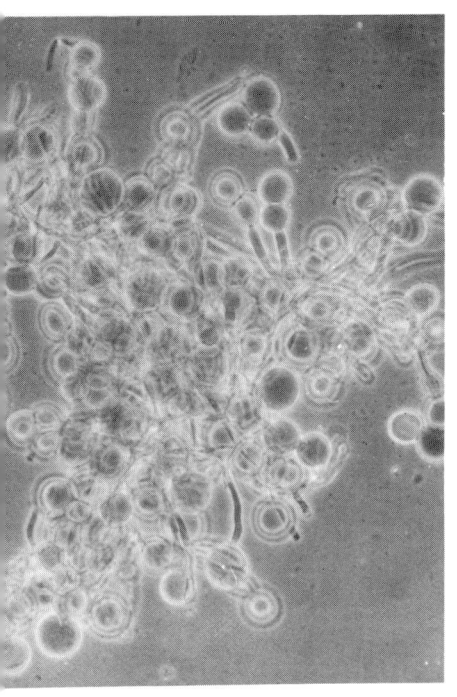

23

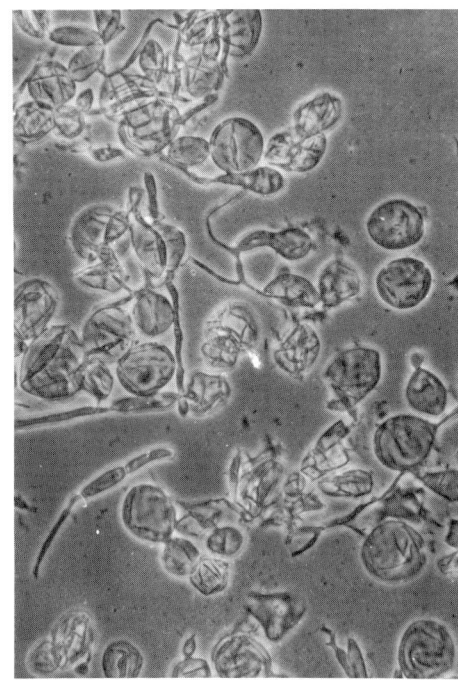

24

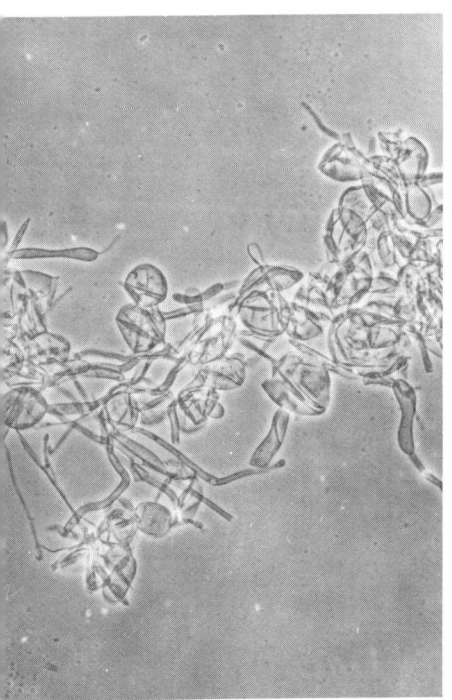

25

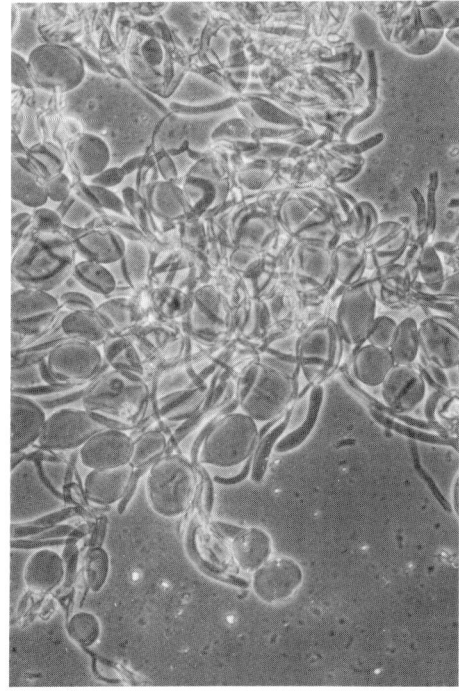

26

Plate 27. Volva of *Amanita muscaria* var. *alba*

Plate 28. Volva of *Amanita muscaria* var. *formasa*

Plate 29. Volva of *Amanita muscaria* var. *flavivolvata*

Plate 30. Volva of *Amanita muscaria* var. *persicina*

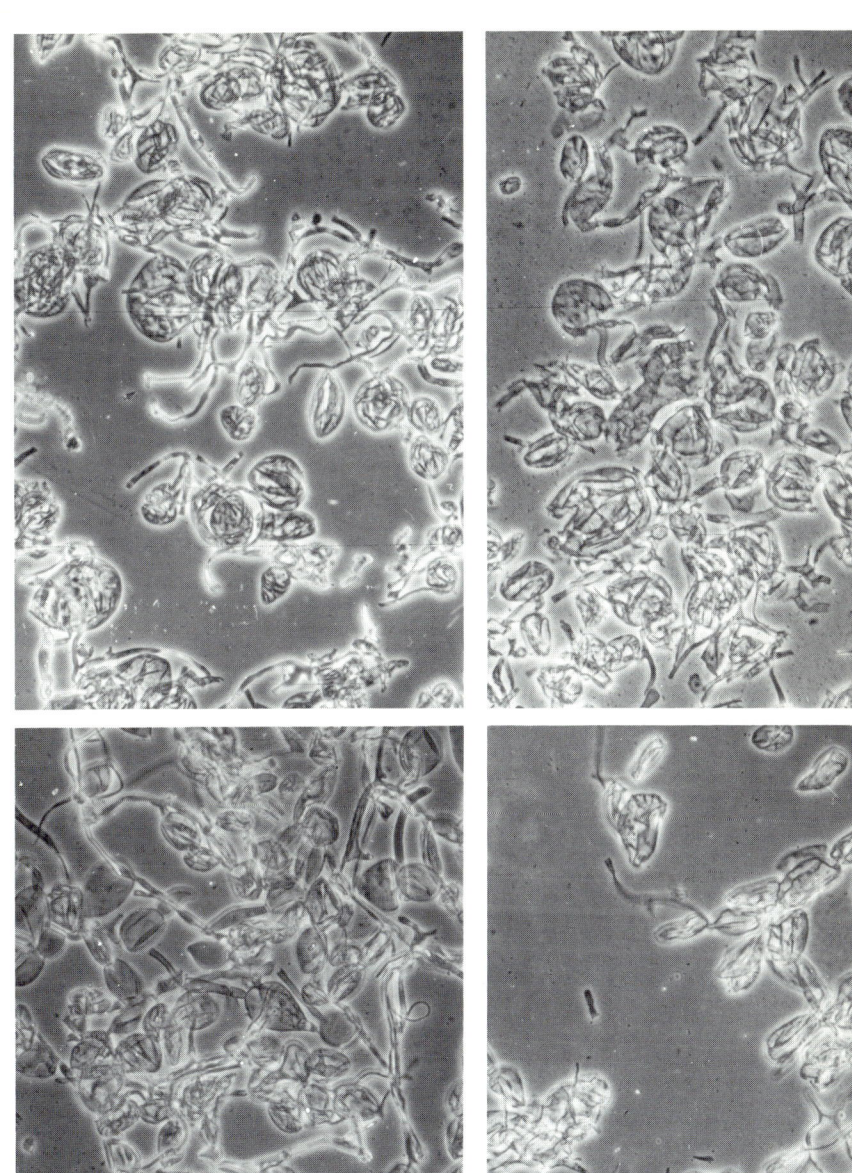

Plate 31. Volva of *Amanita pantherina* var. *pantherina*

Plate 32. Volva of *Amanita pantherina* var. *multisquamosa*

Plate 33. Volva of *Amanita pantherina* var. *velatipes*

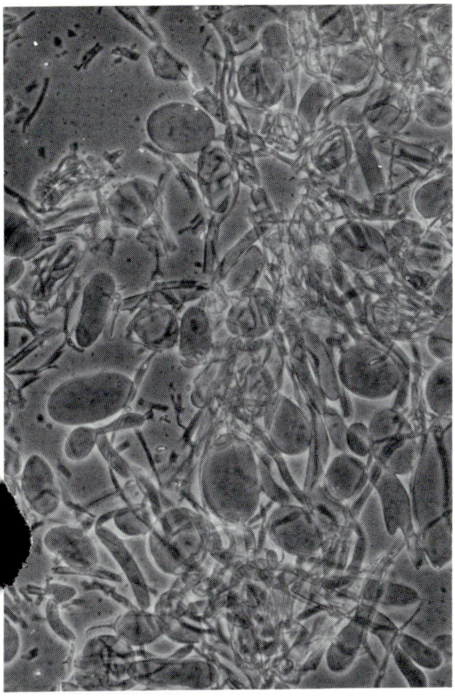

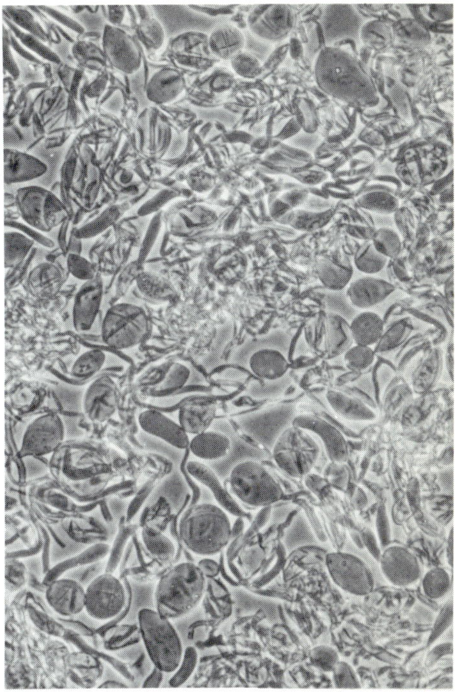

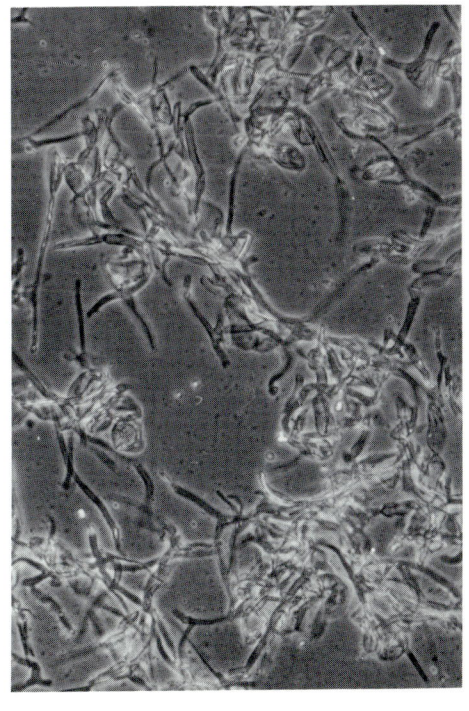

31 32 33

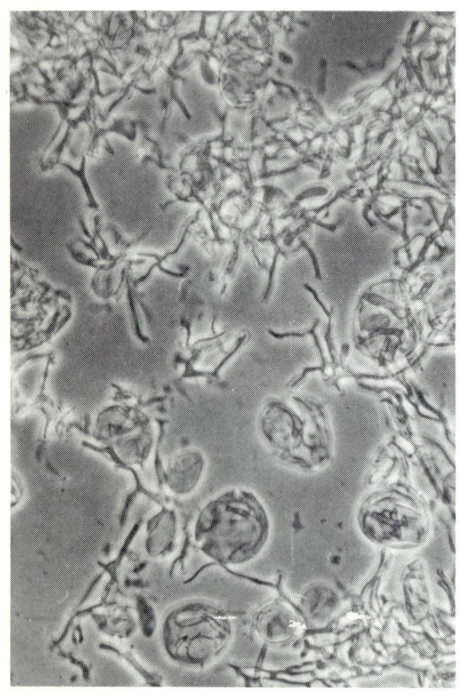 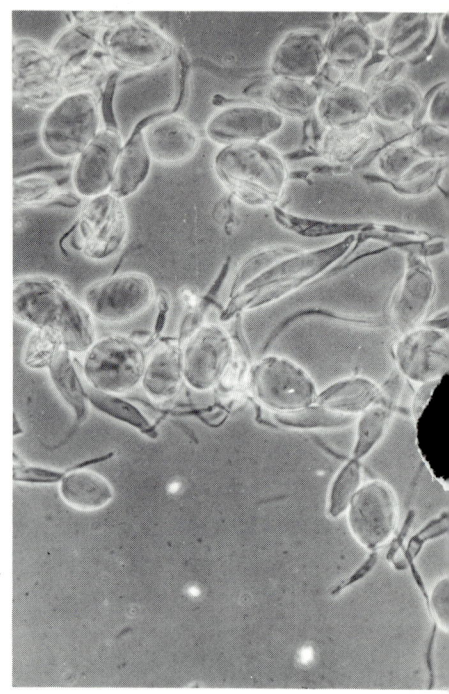

Plate 34. Volva of Amanita parcivolvata

Plate 35. Volva of Amanita wellsii